LIGHT OF ASSISI

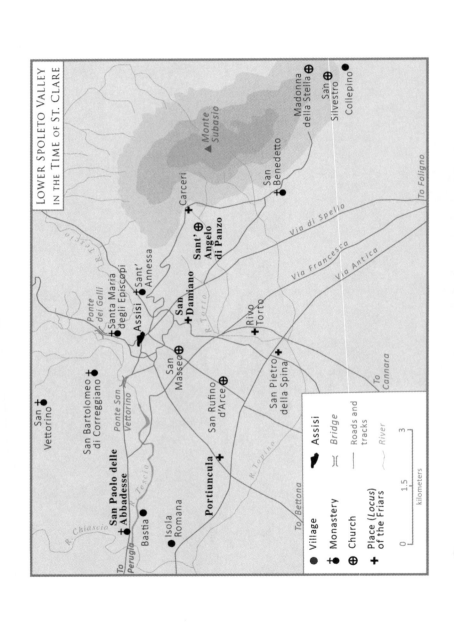

LOWER SPOLETO VALLEY
IN THE TIME OF ST. CLARE

Monte Subasio

Madonna della Stella
San Silvestro
Collepino

Carceri

Sant' Angelo di Panzo

San Benedetto

To Foligno

Via di Spello

Via Francesca

Via Antica

Ponte dei Galli

Sant' Annessa

Santa Maria degli Episcopi

Assisi

San Damiano

R. Tescio

R. Torto

Rivo Torto

To Cannara

San Masseo

San Pietro della Spina

San Rufino d'Arce

R. Topino

To Bettona

San Vettorino

San Bartolomeo di Correggiano

Ponte San Vettorino

R. Tescio

San Paolo delle Abbadesse

Bastia

Isola Romana

Portiuncula

R. Chiascio

To Perugia

●	Village
✚	Monastery
⊕	Church
✚	Place (Locus) of the Friars
▲	Assisi
✕	Bridge
—	Roads and tracks
∿	River

0   1.5   3
kilometers

Light of Assisi

THE STORY OF
Saint Clare

MARGARET CARNEY, OSF

franciscan
media®
Cincinnati, Ohio

Quotations of the writings of Clare and Francis are taken from the following works: *Clare of Assisi, the Lady: Early Documents* (Revised Edition and Translation by Regis J. Armstrong, O.F.M. Cap.), New City Press, 2006. *Francis of Assisi, The Saint, Early Documents, Volume I (1999) and Francis of Assisi, the Founder, Volume II (2000)* Editors: Regis J. Armstrong, O.F.M. Cap., J.A. Wayne Hellmann, O.F.M. Conv., William J. Short, O.F.M. New City Press. Used with permission.

Unless otherwise noted, Scripture texts in this work are taken from the *New American Bible, revised edition* © 2010, 1991, 1986, 1970 Confraternity of Christian Doctrine, Washington, D.C. and are used by permission of the copyright owner. All Rights Reserved. No part of the *New American Bible* may be reproduced in any form without permission in writing from the copyright owner.

LIBRARY OF CONGRESS CATALOGING-IN-PUBLICATION DATA
Names: Carney, Margaret, author.
Title: Light in Assisi : the story of Saint Clare / Margaret Carney.
Description: Cincinnati, Ohio : Franciscan Media, [2021] | Includes bibliographical references. | Summary: "This book will introduce St. Clare of Assisi to those who do not know her and those who wish to know her better. It leads the reader from Clare's birth to her death. While taking account of modern scholarship, Sr. Margaret Carney tells the story of this medieval woman in a way readers today can understand"—Provided by publisher.
Identifiers: LCCN 2020052408 (print) | LCCN 2020052409 (ebook) | ISBN 9781632533708 (trade paperback) | ISBN 9781632533715 (ebook)
Subjects: LCSH: Clare, of Assisi, Saint, 1194-1253. | Christian women saints—Italy—Assisi—Biography. | Christian saints—Italy—Assisi—Biography. | Assisi (Italy)—Biography.
Classification: LCC BX4700.C6 C3725 2021 (print) | LCC BX4700.C6 (ebook) | DDC 282.092 [B]—dc23
LC record available at https://lccn.loc.gov/2020052408
LC ebook record available at https://lccn.loc.gov/2020052409

Cover and book design by Mark Sullivan
Copyright ©2021, Margaret Carney, OSF. All rights reserved.
ISBN 978-1-63253-370-8

Published by Franciscan Media
28 W. Liberty St.
Cincinnati, OH 45202
www.FranciscanMedia.org

Printed in the United States of America.
Printed on acid-free paper.
22 23 24 25 5 4 3

Dedicated
to
Sheila Carney, RSM,
and
Catherine Blahut, OSF,
with gratitude
for a lifetime of sisterhood

Contents

The purpose of this book is simple: to introduce St. Clare of Assisi to those who do not know her and those who wish to know her better. Long identified as a companion and follower of St. Francis of Assisi, she has suffered the inevitable overshadowing of the enormous stature of Francis among Christian saints and religious geniuses. European experts in early Franciscan history have long worked on important projects that preserved and extended our knowledge of St. Clare. The English-speaking reader was, however, rarely able to find sufficient material to have an accurate picture of her. In the last fifty years that has changed. What was at first a small trickle of studies of her spirituality has turned into a steady stream of important works. A number of biographical studies emerged at the time of her 800th centenary in 1993. The most important contributions are the volumes that have given us excellent translations of her writings, primitive biographies, and related documents from the thirteenth and fourteenth centuries. Other publications of an academic nature help us discover more of the historical context or theological underpinnings of her writings. Finally, we also now have a wealth of poetry, music, art, and theatrical offerings to enrich her portrait. What has been missing in the midst of this rising tide of materials is a biography that can lead a reader from her birth to her death, simply telling her story while taking account of modern scholarship. That is what this book tries to do.

Here are some key notions for you to keep in mind as you read.

The book does not ask the reader to master the intricacies of the many debates that currently occupy experts in Franciscan and medieval history.

The book tries to avoid interpretations that represent contemporary culture and sensibilities but would not have figured in Clare's thoughts or decisions. It is important to bring contemporary insight to the topic and every scholar or artist will inevitably do so. However, it is also important to avoid overstating interpretations that simply could not have existed in her time and place.

The book works to weave the threads of Clare's story with that of Francis, but it also gives due importance to the long stretch of years that followed his death—years in which Clare's position in the Franciscan world was of great significance.

The book is her *story*. It is the task of scholars to critique each other's work, to forge ahead to solve unanswered questions, and to keep an open mind—always ready to abandon an old and deficient answer for a new and more trustworthy one. A storyteller has to decide which of many possible interpretations can be incorporated into her narrative. Story has one function; history has another. I have tried to honor current scholarship and indicate instances—usually by posing a question—in which there may still be important discoveries to be made. (Of course, some colleagues will argue with my choices and I beg their indulgence from the start.)

The book is an attempt to provide an answer to the many women and men who have asked why we know so little about Clare when we have such an "embarrassment of riches" in the countless biographies of St. Francis.

Method

A few words about method may be useful.

The place names are given in their Italian form as they are designated today by the people of Assisi. Where there is a question of spelling for proper names, the Italianate spelling has been used.

The word Rule is spelled variously with a capital R designating a text now formally identified by its author's name in our sources. The terms "form of life" and "rule" are interchanged at times.

The quotations from the sources are few in number and readers are encouraged to use those sources. They are found in the following volumes:

Clare of Assisi, the Lady: Early Documents. (Revised Edition and Translation by Regis J. Armstrong, O.F.M. Cap.). New City Press, 2006.

Francis of Assisi, The Saint. Early Documents, Volume I (1999) and Francis of Assisi, the Founder, Volume II (2000). Editors: Regis J. Armstrong, O.F.M. Cap., J.A. Wayne Hellmann, O.F.M. Conv., William J. Short, O.F.M. New City Press.

Meaning

I made Clare's acquaintance while writing a doctoral thesis about her Rule. From that experience thirty years ago, I understand that Clare offers two extraordinarily important lessons. The first is obvious. It is the recognition of how important women—and this woman in particular—are to the Franciscan story. The second is more subtle. It is the lesson that Clare's importance stems from the fact that she was the recipient of a powerful charism of her own—a gift bestowed by the Spirit of the Lord and given to her in a fullness and forcefulness that was hers alone. That charism, matched with the equally full and forceful charism of Francis, created something akin to nuclear fission. It unleashed a mighty power of example and of hope for people who wanted to live the authentic Christian message. Too often we suppose that our study and imitation of these great saints is a sure path to our own beatitude. Her story shows us that what matters is not the effort to "draw down" from the spiritual wealth of others whom we admire as though only a supplicant's sharing of another's gift can make us good. What she shows us is that we need only have the courage to unlock what is within us, to spend our days powered by the graced anointing that we already possess.

I

THE OFFREDUCCIO FAMILY

Assisi is a postage stamp of a town. It sits on a plateau wedged into the side of Mount Subasio, the mountain that towers over the valley of Spoleto. At dawn and eventide its pale stone walls shimmer, paying a grateful homage of light and warmth to the sun. It is, in the words of the poet Alfred Noyes, "the mountain's castled crown." It was here that a child, Chiara, was born to a noble family in 1193 or 1194. Her father was Favarone di Offreducio. Her mother's name was Ortulana. The newest member of a powerful clan, her complete "title" would require recognition of three generations: Chiara di Favarone di Offreducio di Bernardino. While praying for a safe delivery, Ortulana heard a Voice assuring her that this child was destined to be a great light. In translation, this name by which she would be known in centuries to come was Clare. Today we know her as St. Clare of Assisi.

The City

When the baby Clare was "carried to the light"— the Italian idiom for being born—she enlarged a family that was a mirror of the changing ways of medieval society. She was a native of Assisi. From Roman times this town had enjoyed a position of military advantage close to the Via Flaminia. It boasted the residence of Properzio, one of the great poets of Roman antiquity. On the western slope of the mountain are the barely visible remains of the Roman amphitheater, and the well of an ancient Roman cistern forms the base of the cathedral's tower. The most dramatic emblem of this lost civilization stands in the center of the Piazza del Commune, the central plaza of the city. It is the Temple of Minerva, an arresting site that captures Assisi's ancient pedigree in stone.

In time, Assisi, with the rest of the empire, became a place of Christian habitation. The citizens honored the memory of their martyred bishop, Rufino. His remains were contained in a Roman sarcophagus preserved in the cathedral. Clare grew up observing the ongoing construction of a new cathedral of San Rufino on a small plateau above the main market area of the town. In that same upper region of the city were the homes and protective towers of the nobility. The young Clare and her family would be able to witness and participate in many an ecclesiastical event and celebration by simply crossing the threshold of the family manor.

Still, another church—an abbey—played a role in Assisi's Christian culture. The large Benedictine monastery that crowned Mount Subasio supported smaller "plants" of monastic dwellings in the city and in the valley below. These monks provided important services such as reclamation of arable land in the valley. This agricultural improvement added to the prosperity of the town. From the monks the people also learned the possibilities of literacy and of the preservation of knowledge from past civilizations. Their permanence and position communicated a life of remarkable sustainability, order, and security based on love of God and neighbor. These were some of the strengths of Assisi.

Weaknesses abounded as well. The church's clergy—those not in monastic orders—lacked even modest levels of theological education. They were not capable of meeting the needs of people awakening to a new social identity. Issues of greed, armed conflict, and class struggle arose. The allure of the primitive Christian message was shared by new companies of preachers and lay reformers. While some of these evangelists came from the monasteries, increasingly it was lay men and, sometimes, lay women who claimed the right to lead a renewal of Christian practice. Tired of a church that did not respond to the emerging shape of society, these daring reformers took matters into their own hands. Such bravado was sure to be an affront to the power of the papacy. When such confrontations took place, they rarely ended peacefully. The price for daring to call out the scandals of the church's clergy or hierarchy was, at the worst, death and at the least, excommunication.

The men of Clare's family belonged to the upper strata of society; the shorthand name for them was the *maiores*. They were the "major league" members. Their rights to create laws and impose them on people of lower classes had been unquestioned for centuries. Their power came from military conquest combined with ownership of vast lands. They had a monopoly on the right to determine financial policies and just about every other form of social regulation. For the *maiores*, property was constantly increased through marriages that brought more land and goods under the family's control. All needs were met within the closed system of the castle and its various levels of inhabitants from the lord to the farm laborer.

Something new, however, was occurring in both small towns and larger cities. Certain workers outside of the feudal compounds were becoming important to local prosperity. Such was the merchant. He stood outside the magic circle of the castle's denizens. He made it possible for people to get goods, trade, and sell produce even though he (or she) lacked powerful royal connections. This group was dubbed the *minores*, the "lesser ones" in contrast to their noble neighbors. These men and women gradually recognized their own growing role in local prosperity. When the upper-class leaders tried to rig local policies and prices to their own advantage, the *minores* exercised their own leverage and insisted on being included in political and economic decision-making. The *maiores* were in no hurry to invite them into "the room where it happened," but signs were everywhere that soon a new framework would have to be created.

Such was the city that was home to St. Clare.

The Family

What do we know about her family? The family was described by early Franciscan biographers in terms of power and prestige. They were one of the family systems comprised not of a nucleus of husband, wife, and children but of a small corporation (consortium) of families. Such a consortium was a network of male heirs linked by negotiated marriages, and economic and military cooperation. Her family counted seven knights who formed a powerful league with their properties, servants, and troops. Clare's father was Favarone di Offreduccio di Bernardino. He was one of five brothers and he was simply described as a soldier. The absence of fuller descriptions bedevils all who wish to know more of her story. His memory is never expanded in the earliest biographies. The obligations of the consortium or the call of the Crusades may have shaped his life. He fathered three daughters—Clare, Catherine, and Beatrice—but it seems he was already deceased by the time Clare reached the age of eighteen.

Clare's uncle Monaldo was the family's patriarch. The archives of the diocese contain a letter on which one of the signatures is that of Clare's grandfather, Bernardino. The letter assures the bishop that the family tower will not exceed the height of the new cathedral then under construction. The tower—a normal feature of the large palazzo of a nobleman—was a status symbol and a structure for safety in times of war. This agreement between Bernardino and his bishop mirrored the constant interplay of powerful leaders who lived in the upper reaches—the *parte de sopra*—of the growing town. They worked to manage peaceful solidarity within their ranks.

Clare's mother, Ortulana, came of noble stock. Women of her station were prepared to lead a large household, raise its children, and care for its inhabitants in terms of food, clothing, health care, and domestic training. When the husband or master of the house was absent for military or commercial ventures it fell to her to keep the extended household and its affairs in good order. The name Ortulana evokes images of gardens and planting, since it echoes the Italian term for an orchard or garden—*orto*. Her strength of character and willpower are evident in the fact that she made three major pilgrimages: St. Peter's in Rome, St. Michael's shrine in southern Italy, and the Holy Land. Such rigorous travel allowed women a singular opening to a world beyond the walls of home and city. Yet, we should not assume that such journeys were simply a way to experience a world beyond one's narrow walls. The pilgrimage—especially to Jerusalem—was the ultimate expression of a spirit of profound penance, of atonement for sins. We may ask for what—or for *whom*—was Lady Ortulana driven to this heroic travel?

How did Ortulana raise her three daughters? In addition to Clare, she and Favarone had two other girls: Beatrice and Catherine. The profound religious stamp she created in her daughters' lives may well owe a great deal to the pilgrimages. We can imagine nights filled with tales of her travels. Hers were stories of encounters with fellow pilgrims, the dangers of the road and the sea, the allure of markets and bazaars in foreign cities, the joy and awe of reaching the inner sanctum of a holy shrine. She would have taught them about the graces given to those who persevered in such penitential dedication and the importance of a life guided by faith in company with others fired by the same desires.

Uprisings and Exile

The family's importance became its liability when an uprising of the *minores* of Assisi forced these nobles into exile for safety. This flight took place in 1200. The adopted home of the Offreducio family was Perugia. There, together with like-minded *maiores*, they made common cause with their Perugia hosts. This required the Assisi nobles to swallow their pride and pledge loyalty to the city they had long considered an enemy. This adoptive citizenship provided safe harbor for these important families. It also created bonds among households that would play a role in Clare's future life. These intimate connections of kinship, social status and political alliance would form part of the enduring pattern of her life. Unlike her mother, her travels would be limited and likely few and far between. Yet, within this circumscribed life she drew upon relationships with women of substance from both Perugia and Assisi. They were destined to become her companions in a daring evangelical adventure.

The resolution of the protracted division between "upper" Assisi—now in league with Perugia—and "lower" Assisi was an armed battle. Conducted on the broad plain of the valley that separated the two hill towns, it is known by the small hamlet where the action took place: Collestrada. Assisi suffered humiliating defeat. The survivors of its troops became prisoners. Now the way was finally clear for the nobles in exile to return home.

Within this tangle of events we find the first intersection of the lives of Clare and Francis of Assisi. The forces that made the flight to Perugia necessary for the Offreducio clan were set in motion by the newly powerful *minores* of Assisi—the group to which the family of Francis Bernardone belonged. Francis, a partisan in the battle to reinforce the claims of the *minores*, was taken prisoner and jailed in Perugia. In this small slice of time we find both Clare and Francis experiencing an unhappy confinement in Perugia. Both experience the horrible outcomes of armed battles, of powerful vendettas. Was there an alternative road by which one might travel life's pilgrimage?

But let us pause at this point to learn more of the story of Francis di Bernardone.

Chapter Two

THE BERNARDONE FAMILY

*F*rancis di Bernardone was born in Assisi and baptized Giovanni (John) in 1182. His father was absent at the time of his birth. When he returned home, he insisted on giving his first-born a new name: Francesco—the "French one." Meant to convey the spirit of freedom and enterprise of Pietro's French business associates, it became a prophecy of one destined to open new freedoms to countless generations. But we get ahead of our story.

The Family Business
Pietro was a successful cloth merchant with significant land holdings around the city. Pietro was, perhaps, a relative newcomer to this place. Pietro's wife, Pica, was—some believe—a native of France. Francis and his brother, Angelo, enjoyed generous parenting supported by a promising future for the family business. It is not easy to get an accurate picture of his parents' temperaments. Early biographers chose to portray them in dark tones. They appeared as befuddled folks unable to really appreciate this God-given son of theirs. The indications we have, however, studied without prejudice, show that they were, if anything, indulgent and loving until Francis's religious crisis created unforeseen tensions among them.

From his earliest years, Francis possessed a quickness of imagination and quality of character that made him appear older than his years. As he grew into young manhood, he exhibited a fascinating combination of traits. He was at once generous to the poor and extravagant with his drinking buddies. He loved fine outfits, banquets, and hijinks in the city streets at night. A legend grew that portrayed the young man being honored in the town plaza by a pilgrim who passed through one day. The stranger threw his cloak at the feet of Francis and declared in the hearing of all that one day, Francis would be honored in all the world. While the story has been relegated to the status of folklore, the proud ambitions of Pietro were likely not too far down the scale from those of this legendary "prophesying pilgrim."

While his social standing was in a comfortable zone between peasant and prince, Francis conducted himself as though "born to the purple" of his betters. He may have travelled to France with his father. He developed a courtly sensibility that reflected the culture of the troubadours. This flowering of courtesy and honorable conduct was creating new manners and morals throughout the royal households of Europe. The music that embodied these lofty emotions and ideals captured Francis's imagination. Later he would style himself as God's troubadour.

For all of his admiration of a life of nobility, Francis was ensconced in a lucrative mercantile business. The availability of new fabrics and rich Oriental imports made dress not merely a matter of modesty and safety, but a sign of wealth, of social importance. The cloth merchant's role supported the changing ambitions of various subsets of people within a commune. In addition, as a merchant he was part of the various political changes by which the *minores* won respect for their economic value and gained a voice in commercial deliberations. This was the school in which the young Francis learned of virtue and vice, charity and greed.

Military Ambition

While a future in the family trade was assured to him, Francis longed to earn the title of a knight. Such ambition was not delusional. A man of modest origins could, in fact, earn that rank if he had sufficient money, equipment, and victory in battle. Such was his hope in entering two military ventures. In the first, he joined the losing side when he took part in the Battle of Collestrada. Taken hostage, he languished in prison until the ransom was paid.

When he returned home, it was obvious that the imprisonment had taken a terrible toll. His recovery was slow. Beyond his physical weakness, Francis suffered from a loss of sense of purpose, of joy. The escapades of his short military career had exposed the ugly face of death. He witnessed the brutal end of many of his companions. While stories of the term in prison portray him as the cheerful voice in the crowd of despairing POWs, he did not emerge unscarred. He appeared to have lost direction.

He decided to try a second time to demonstrate his military valor. Just one year after his release from prison, he joined the army of Walter of Brienne who was waging a crusading campaign in southern Italy. Hardly had he begun the trip, when a strange dream directed him to give up his plan to serve a master of arms and enter instead into the service of the Master, Christ. He obeyed this mysterious command. Returning home to Assisi with no rational explanation for his change of heart, he began the tortured path to discern the will of God for his life.

From Prison to Penitence

He worked in the family shop alongside his father and brother, Angelo. His sudden fits of sadness, his excessive donations to beggars, his disappearing into mountain caves to pray—this behavior caused anxiety and aggravation in the Bernardone household. Little by little, the distance between his father's hopes and the unpredictable actions of the veteran son became a wall between them.

Dramatic encounters pulled Francis more and more into a sense of being called to a radical choice. He met a leper on the plain below Assisi and instead of taking flight, he embraced the sufferer and was filled with a spirit of joy. He had encountered Jesus in one who was the poorest of the poor. While travelling home from making a sale in neighboring Foligno, he went into the abandoned chapel of San Damiano that stood outside the city walls of Assisi. There a Byzantine cross hung over the altar. The face of Christ gazed at him with serenity and compassion. Then he heard a Voice calling him to repair the ruined church. He left his sale proceeds there for the resident priest and began to spend time in actual repair work on the old structure.

Between these moments of vision and voices he continued a suffering search for his way forward. He adopted the way of life of a public penitent. This was a form of religious dedication based on the Church's ancient rules for atoning for one's sins. The disciplines included prayer, dressing in sackcloth, fasting, making a pilgrimage, and offering one's service to those in need. It could extend for a lifetime, but it could also be temporary under the instruction of one's confessor or bishop. Bishop Guido of Assisi understood what Francis was doing and found himself drawn into the task of guarding this fledgling disciple.

As time went on the break with Pietro and the business created a public scandal. His father could no longer abide the antics of a son who squandered the money Pietro worked so hard to provide. Threats, being "grounded" within the family home, pleas and prayers were to no avail. Pietro made plans to force the issue by suing his son for the return of his property. A trial was arranged with the bishop presiding. There Francis publicly renounced his paternal inheritance, stripped himself in the presence of the citizens, and declared himself now obedient to a Heavenly Father. Bishop Guido wrapped the naked Francis in his mantle. By this sign of ecclesial protection, the bishop helped inaugurate a new era, one that would unfold rapidly and end up making Assisi a revered name in all of Christendom.

Over a period of years, perhaps six or seven in all, Francis gradually discovered a dramatic and original conception of how Christian life must be lived in its fullness. He would follow "in the footprints of Jesus" with every fiber of his being. That.... and nothing more. What made his plan unique was its insistence on total poverty, total lack of permanent resources of any kind. This ideal was one espoused by early Christians. For Francis it not only reflected a profound sense of the humility of the Son of God, it allowed physical freedom to go where needs were greatest. Earning his way as a day laborer he became entwined with others of the *minores*—including the working poor. This "novitiate" brought him to intimate knowledge of the needs and hopes of the townspeople. He learned to speak their language— quite literally.

The second hallmark of his activity was his focus on peace-making. He refused to denounce the heretics, preferring instead to offer clear Gospel teaching. He made the verbal greeting of "peace" a daily part of his encounters, even when that language garnered ridicule and rough treatment. His sword was beaten, not into a ploughshare, but into a preaching style that captivated those who heard him call for the end of violence of all kinds.

As this new way unfolded within him and was mirrored in his every word and action, the early seasons of public rejection melted into a new sense of wonder and respect among those witnessing the change. Other men sought to join him and search with him for the way to be authentic companions of Jesus. The attraction crossed lines of social status. One of these early recruits was Rufino, one of the younger knights of the Offreducio clan and a cousin of Clare. The defection of such a promising young man to the band of preaching vagabonds must have created a furor. The bishop of Assisi seems to have been guided by an exceptional ability to see the inner truth of what Francis and the first brothers were after. He gave his support and never wavered even when the sanity of the project was in doubt.

Francis moved in and out of various settings during these years. He had shelter in monasteries, churches, and hospices. He observed the way in which others tried to rid the Church of its sins by "scorched earth" preaching crusades. He encountered sincere seekers who suffered to bring about the lessons of the Gospel to towns and markets. He also encountered those who had long since abandoned any loyalty to the Church. These heretics, the Cathars and Waldensians, were taking many wearied folks with them into a wilderness of erroneous teachings and unorthodox rituals. Francis's conviction about following Jesus with utter simplicity was joined to a conviction that he must keep faith with the Church. Flawed it might be, but it was the human container of all the truths that could lead one to God's divine truth. Francis's simple message of peace and penance struck a new and enticing chord in Assisi and the towns of the region.

Finally, in 1209, with eleven other men joining him, Francis approached the papal court in Rome seeking formal permission to live according to the Gospel with no other "rule" of life. Innocent III, brilliant administrator and lawyer that he was, allowed himself to be convinced to give this upstart preacher from Umbria a chance. That chance, given with some hesitation and with the instruction to continue being accountable to the See of Peter, was all Francis needed. A papal *fiat* opened the door to an unimaginable future.

Chapter Three

EDUCATION AND ENCOUNTERS

With the passage of time (and the promulgation of new peace pacts), the Offreducio clan returned to Assisi. Clare, now a young adolescent, resumed the sheltered life of unmarried girls within the walls of her native city and the confines of her home. There she continued to advance in native abilities and new skills. When the time came, her marriage would install her in a household of substance. This was her destiny and the family would prepare her to embrace it. What might make up the curriculum for such a promising young woman?

A Young Woman's World

From her own writings and the writings of others, we see evidence of her education. She possessed a fine level of literacy. The mere fact of being literate—capable of reading and writing— was an extraordinary achievement for women at the time. Her biographers make a point of telling us that she was eager to hear the kind of sermon that exhibited theological depth. This fact probably indicates that she, like so many women denied a formal education, actually possessed an intellectual capacity equal to that of the men with whom she would work.

We have many testimonies about Clare's healing gifts. While a number of miraculous cures are described, we also see instances in which her prayers are accompanied by ordinary remedies that she offers to those in need. She may have had a solid foundation in the medicinal arts. Women had responsibility for the health of their households in good times and bad. Each generation transmitted recipes for remedies and herbal medications. Add to this basic instruction a special talent for nursing and Clare gave evidence of possessing that set of gifts.

Her protracted and successful negotiations with ecclesiastical dignitaries reveal a talent for conflict management and high-level diplomatic negotiations. Was she party to debates among her uncles about political alliances, peace treaties, and new communal agreements? Did she observe the various ways in which those of noble stock conducted negotiations and the manner in which women conducted themselves as the mediators within these large extended families? We cannot say for certain, but it is evident that she possessed significant talent for bargaining with the powerful men in her life.

There are many indications of Clare's skill with needle and thread. She engaged in spinning cloth even when confined to her bed. She may, in fact, have developed this ability over the years along with other sisters in the community. The many instances that describe her working with her hands include common menial tasks. She did not shrink from taking her turn with the lowest assignments. For the sisters she was a teacher, a manager, and a disciplinarian. She was destined to run a noble household and had the formation that was required for such a role. That her talents would become the cornerstone of a very different kind of household was a providential surprise still to come.

Early biographies extol the piety and generosity she exhibited in her youngest years. While such praise was common in telling the stories of saints, the evidence of her early behavior contrasts sharply with that of Francis whose youth was clearly a patchwork of light and shadow. She, on the other hand, adopted practices of penance that were extraordinary for one so young. She wore a penitential garment, recited prayers regularly, and saved her food for the poor. One interesting detail is that she sent alms to men working at Santa Maria degli Angeli, the tiny Marian sanctuary in the valley. This church, also called the Portiuncula, was the rallying point of the early generation of brothers. Was this, perhaps, the first evidence we have of a desire to support the companions of Francis, among whom was her cousin, Rufino?

While women might be married as early as the age of fifteen, once a woman reached eighteen, the marriage plan moved into high gear. The family initiated the period of courtship. To its chagrin, Clare rejected more than one suitor. During the investigation for her canonization one of these rejected suitors, Raineri di Bernardo, gave his testimony. Clare rejected his multiple offers of marriage. Instead, she urged him to join her in seeking a life of dedication to Christ. A man whose proposal she rejected carried that memory for forty years but lived to swear to her holiness and help insure her speedy canonization.

It was becoming obvious to anxious family leaders that Clare had already decided that her life would not follow the expected path. She was strongly set upon another route whose contours were as yet unclear. This time of testing in the crucible of family pressure showed that she possessed a singular sense of self, a self already captivated by a summons from beyond earth's kingdoms.

The Friars

By the time Clare reached the age of marriage, the new frater-nity surrounding Francis di Bernardone was already famous for its charismatic appeal to the masses of Christians in the region and beyond. The men who joined Francis in the earliest days endured with him the scorn of the town. Little by little, though, that scorn turned to cautious admiration and finally to enthusi-astic endorsement. People were drawn by the new solidarity that these men exhibited with the *minores*. With them they showed a willingness to join daily in tough and menial work, the sim-plicity of sharing all things and offering protection for the most vulnerable. These attributes began to exert a magnetic pull on public opinion. These brothers also spoke of living from the pages of the Gospel of Jesus in a way that no priest or prelate had ever done. They appeared on fire with a love of God that did not seek escape into the monastic enclosures but found its way right into the heart of the piazza and the marketplace. Their speech was not the language of bishops and university experts, but the common speech of ordinary people. They were part of a generation moving from a Latin vocabulary and grammar to new dialects of a country, a region. It was a language both famil-iar and eminently practical and these pilgrim brothers did not hesitate to use it for holy ends.

The brothers were no longer limited to Assisi as a field of action. In fact, they were travelling to many cities to offer the good news that had drawn them away from the follies of ava-rice and armed vendettas. As their message transfixed crowds in town after town, numbers of young men sought to join them. Women were no less inspired. For some women, the choice of a life dedicated to works of mercy and prayer in small households was already a possibility. Such households existed in many towns and were made up of widows and other women dedicated to chastity or virginity. Such households might enjoy the patronage of powerful families or of a commune as a whole. This patronage would be gladly offered in exchange for the social help for the sick, pilgrims, or beggars provided by these dedicated ladies. How such women acquired and maintained their knowledge of the Gospels, of church teachings, would depend upon local bishops or monasteries.

As the friars exerted their evangelical influence wherever they went, women, especially those already seeking an authentic life of Christian discipline, became part of the growing movement. The "new springtime" of reform and revitalization that Francis inspired needed to give these women a place.

Encounters with Francis

In Assisi, the knowledge that Clare was rejecting marriage proposals and that she seemed bent on a religious path was becoming a matter of public speculation. We do not know when the first encounter between Clare and Francis took place. Since her home stood beside the Cathedral of San Rufino, she could have heard him preach there. His frequent preaching appointments inside the city walls stirred a universal interest. The friars were never far away physically. And we can well imagine that they were never far from conversation—whether of argument or admiration. After all, among the earliest to enlist (in addition to Rufino) were Bernard of Quintavalle, an attorney, and Sylvester, a priest of the diocese. Clare breathed the very air that was filled with the new evangelical energy of Francis.

For his part, Francis clearly knew Clare's reputation, the beautiful woman who was irritating the Offreducio patriarchs with her delaying tactics during courtship. The reputation of her saintly mother and of this exceptionally pious daughter would not have been a secret to a native of Assisi. Had her kindness to the workers at Santa Maria touched him personally? Could she be the answer to his prayers about how to answer the women who wanted to participate in this new movement of Gospel living?

Both parties were drawn to seek each other out to discern the stirrings of grace they shared. Did Rufino broker their first meeting? Clare's need to choose a path of Gospel fidelity had become urgent. These meetings were carefully orchestrated. Clare was accompanied by an older companion, Bona di Guelfuccio, a friend and family servant. Such precaution was standard practice for an unmarried woman conversing with a man outside the home. The meetings were secret since Clare was determined to avoid family scrutiny. The brief condensation of their encounters stresses Francis's effort to woo her on behalf of the Divine Bridegroom, whose troubadour and liege man he was. Another brother, Philip, was Francis's companion and no less persuasive in his entreaties.

Little by little her desire to join them grew. Equally important, the brothers' conviction that Clare's calling was of divine origin grew apace. When her resolve to commit herself to this life— a life that Francis was leading in dramatic new fashion— was assured, the conversation turned to tactical planning. What resulted was an escape from Assisi and family, a formal induction into the ranks of women vowed to virginity, and the search for a stable place for women among the first Franciscans.

Chapter Four

MIDNIGHT EXODUS

Since her plans with Francis were formulated in secrecy, the means by which Clare's actual departure from her house and the city had to be carefully orchestrated. There were important contingencies to manage. The year was 1212. On Palm Sunday morning she attended the Mass in the cathedral. There, along with the other young women, she appeared in her best clothes. This ritual of dressing up for the first of the springtime feasts was a well-known custom. Francis explicitly encouraged her to don her best wardrobe when she appeared in the cathedral. His flair for the dramatic was on display here as he imagined the sensation that would be created when Clare exchanged that glamourous costume the next day for the drab garb of a penitent.

During the service in the cathedral, Clare did not process to the bishop to receive the palm from him. Instead, she remained where she was, and he moved into the body of the church to bring her the blessed branch. Much speculation has surrounded this odd bit of the story. At least one interpretation is that the bishop, in handing her the branch, secretly signified his approval and that all her plans had his blessing.

Late that same night, Clare left her home on the piazza of San Rufino. Here again, details give rise to interpretations both symbolic and actual. How did she manage to leave without a guard detecting her departure? Years ago, it was popular to describe her as departing from a door known as "the door of the dead." This version relied on the belief that great homes had a door used only for the removal of a corpse. No such doors existed, however, and that appealing bit of theater has been cut from modern accounts. What is likely is that certain doors of large households were not closely guarded at night and one of these permitted a safe exit for her.

The next puzzle was how would she manage to leave by a city gate which would be under guard as well? Here, again, the bishop's collaboration gives the answer. The gate by which she could leave the city after curfew was in a section owned by the bishop—the palm branch might also have served as an "all clear" relative to the route she must take. This Moiano gate was not only a safe option, it was steeped in ancient lore. This portal was dedicated to the Roman god Janus, the deity who faced both to the past and the future. Thus the gate also stood for new beginnings, for changes. Once on the other side of this gate and Assisi's protective walls, she would become a citizen of another "commune" of Gospel striving.

Who accompanied her? While we know the names of women who played key roles as chaperones or companions, here there is only an anonymous co-conspirator. The prospect of two women making the nighttime trek along the winding path from the city walls to the little chapel of Santa Maria is daunting to say the least. Were there, perhaps, some brothers making the trip with them? It would have fit a knightly conception of courtesy to provide such an escort and to make sure that Clare had such protection at that perilous hour.

Finally, she arrived at the tiny church of Santa Maria degli Angeli. Once there, she was formally received by Francis in a carefully orchestrated ritual. Her beautiful clothing was exchanged for a penitent's robe. Francis himself cut her hair—the time-honored tradition for women seeking to leave the world to live by religious vows. A simple veil marked her as given to Christ in a life of virginity. In the presence of the brothers, Clare professed her dedication to Jesus, and, like them, to poverty and their simple rule. All that she once claimed as a member of a noble family was put aside. All that she would become as a woman fixed on God would be accomplished in partnership with them.

Chapter Five:

PENITENT AND PILGRIM

Now "invested," Clare must be taken to a place of safety. She cannot remain among the men lest scandal immediately nullify the new venture. She must anticipate that her uncle and his retainers will try to block her plan. Thus, the arrangement is that she will be harbored for a time in the nearby monastery of San Paolo. Just a short distance away in the same valley, this abbey was protected by specific papal privileges. These regulations make clear that anyone who attempts to harm its religious women will suffer excommunication. Clare takes refuge among these secure Benedictines.

As predicted, her uncle and his band of relatives arrived to demand that she return home. In reply, she entered the chapel, took hold of the altar, and removed her head covering so that the men could see that she had, indeed, been tonsured. The Offreducio rescue squad left furious and humiliated. Once it was clear her decision could not be thwarted, Clare left this monastery and took up residence with a small community of dedicated women. This group was located outside the city near a church on the slopes of the mountainside called Sant'Angelo in Panzo. Now she was with women who did not seek a monastic cloister but a form that combined presence to needy neighbors along with time for prayer and devotion. Increasing numbers of such small houses or "hospices" flourished in central Italy. The nickname given to such women was the "*bizzoche*"— a reference to the wooden sandals they often wore.

While Clare resided at this hospice of Sant'Angelo her sister Catherine decided to follow and join her there. We can only imagine the experience of Catherine as the Offreducio lords rant against her beloved sister and threaten her and the younger Beatrice. Whatever fate Catherine might have imagined for herself, she would not be forced to follow the dictates of her uncle and the other knights. She escaped to the mountain.

The protections afforded at San Paolo are absent at Sant' Angelo. Monaldo can and does violate the precincts of the household and physically captures Catherine to force her retreat. As the men carry her away, they take out their fury in beating her and tearing her hair. A miraculous intervention thwarts their plan. Monaldo and the men find Catherine's body becomes too heavy to carry. His arm is paralyzed as if a stroke is in progress. Defeated again, the men depart, leaving the wounded young woman on the roadside where she will be rescued by Clare and her new companions. The high price of entrance into the Franciscan way of things is increasing daily for the women as once it did for the first male companions. Francis, in accepting Catherine into the company of the brothers and sisters—now plural—decides to confer a new name upon her—Agnes. This choice is prompted by his admiration for her steadfast acceptance of physical suffering as the price to pay for following Jesus. Like the great Roman martyr, she represents a triumph of grace. She teaches the brothers that the "weaker sex" is capable of heroic strength.

San Damiano

Time passes. At last we read that Clare, Catherine—now Agnes—and others already affiliated with them, take up residence in the small monastery attached to the church of San Damiano. This monastery had once served as a waystation for monks working in the valley at a distance that prevented return to the monastery at the top of Mount Subasio on a nightly basis. Now it was under the bishop's jurisdiction. He extends his protection to this newest expression of feminine Christian renewal. He is trusting that his support will not be in vain.

Now Clare and her very first sister companions take up the life they envisioned. San Damiano is outside the city walls on the lower slope of the mountain and close to an ancient mineral spring. It functioned as a refuge for anyone making the ascent into the city but unable to reach it before curfew. It functioned as a place known for healing waters from Roman times. It functioned as a refuge for friars in need of recuperation from illness or exhaustion. It functioned as the place where Clare, the "footprint of the Mother of God," manifests unending feminine compassion to all in need.

Here Clare will live and here Clare will die.

Chapter Six

STONE BY STONE

Clare recalled these new beginnings in later years. That she and her sisters had survived the painful trials of the foundation was not nearly as surprising to her as it was to Francis. "When the blessed Francis saw, however, that although we were physically weak and frail, we did not shirk deprivation, poverty, hard work, trial or the shame or contempt of the world—rather we considered them as great delights, as he had frequently examined us according to the example of the saints and his brothers— he greatly rejoiced in the Lord" (Testament, 27-29). Taking each word of this recollection on its merits, we must imagine that the early years of life in San Damiano were a continual struggle at levels material, social, and spiritual. What was the work like—"day by day, stone by stone"—for the Poor Sisters at the beginning?

Building Slowly

First there was the house-making and housekeeping itself to consider. Establishing a dwelling fit as habitation for a large number of women was, in itself, a monumental task considering the condition of the long-abandoned property. The garden would have to be cultivated anew since in that first year the growing season was already well underway. Whose assistance provided needed supplies before the women could claim a level of self-sufficiency? When they could turn to the task of growing vegetables, fruits, herbs, olive trees—how was this work done? Who among the sisters had the green thumb and capacity to teach the others? How did the brothers help with the heavy tasks of the beginnings?

Given the stress on help for the sick, to whom did the task of preparing ointments, salves, teas, and other remedies fall? Did the small hospice on the hillside gradually acquire the needed containers, instruments, and tools for a well-stocked infirmary? Would sympathetic townsfolk help ensure that this "emergency room" was able to do its work? Friars came for respite and help. Their needs likely produced practical routines of nursing care and convalescent support.

Dormitory furnishings—sparse as they were—had to be acquired or fashioned. They needed bed coverings, blankets, hangings to keep out the constant drafts sweeping down from Subasio's heights. The sisters' clothing had to be procured. Theirs was the plain dress of women of the penitential movement. Did they find these ready for their use? Did they make them or alter clothing given to them by others? Cheap fabric was all that was permitted. A head covering was the norm for all unmarried women. Only later would the details of a religious habit become standardized with directions on how it would be worn and what liberties could or could not be taken with its use.

Preparing meals required considerable appliances: pots, ladles, cauldrons, knives, storage vessels, ovens. Where did the supply of firewood come from? While fasting was a constant regimen, prudent balancing of food intake was part of the monastic tradition. Clare would later advise her friend, Agnes of Prague, to see to it that sisters did not harm themselves by excessive fasting. (This was advice she gave but did not follow it herself.) Clearly, they needed dishware, drinking cups, serving platters.

Maintaining cleanliness was one way to manage the conditions of poor diet and poor protection from the elements. Sanitation measures had to be handled and solutions found when any type of infestation occurred. These chores—the most noisome in a large community—were shared and Clare herself was not above taking her turn.

The physical exertion was enormous; there is little doubt that mental exertions were considerable as well. Many of these women were raised with servants who performed menial chores. Now at San Damiano they had to do this work. And they had to do it amidst constant reminders that family members and former friends regarded their choice as madness. Surely the "runaway brides" felt the sting of public scorn and knew the knife wound of vile jokes and ugly threats. Only by creating a narrative that portrayed them as women deranged and deluded by Francis could the townspeople of Assisi, Spello, or Perugia insulate themselves from the powerful message of the Poor Sisters. Their rejection of life as pawns in the chess game of communal power and greed was not an easy message to accept. Clare remembers that the sisters endured "shame and the contempt of the world." This was no poetic flight of fancy. It was a simple and sad truth.

Did the sisters care for the lepers housed in the valley below during this early period? In time, the laws of cloister would make this impossible, but it may have been one of the tasks of those earliest years. Whether or not the sisters themselves made the trek to the leprosaria, we might imagine that they supplied salves, bandages, and other necessities for the brothers who did go there. What is clear is that others in need of medical expertise came regularly to the Poor Sisters' hospice for ordinary—and sometimes miraculous—help.

Gaining Christ

Sustaining them in these trials was the work of prayer. To such communities the church entrusted the "office" of praying the liturgy of the hours. The day—and night—was punctuated by formal prayer. In this way hymns, psalms, and prayers—recited or sung—would continually rise from earth to heaven. In this way the glory of God never ceased to be celebrated and the needs of humankind never ceased to be a source of trusting petitions.

If those first sisters did, indeed, count the insults and privations as "great delights" what would explain such joy but the exaltation that flows from a love that "surpasses understanding."

> Whatever gain I had, these I have come to consider as loss because of Christ. ...For his sake I have accepted the loss of all things and I consider them so much rubbish, that I may gain Christ....to know him and the power of his resurrection and sharing his sufferings by being conformed to his death, if somehow I may attain the resurrection of the dead. (Philippians 3: 7-11)

These words of the Apostle Paul took flesh in them. It was through the daily cycle of prayer that such "blessed assurance" grew in them. The rounds of hours of the breviary brought the richness of psalms and Scripture texts into dialogue with their daily tasks. Meditation upon the Byzantine Cross, the adoration of the Eucharist, attending Mass, hearing sermons—all gave new meaning to each day's trials or triumphs. Weaving prayer and productive work created the balance within their hearts and minds that allowed them to keep moving.

The poor sisters lived filled with consolation, with assurance. They dared to believe that promise of Jesus. They were learning that he was true to his word and their joy was, indeed, full and free. They learned to reverse their own standards of judgment in favor of the riddle that calls one to lose life in order to gain it. That women could live without the safety net of approved monastic vows and ample endowments and follow Christ in such literal fashion was news indeed. And the women themselves were the first to understand that.

Chapter Seven

REBUILDING THE CHURCH

A s Clare's small band of sisters expanded, so did the activity of Francis's brothers. Preaching themes of Christian conversion and peace-making, they gradually found a decrease in the initial hostility they provoked. Large numbers of men joined them. The brothers were reaching out to towns and villages all over Italy. Francis provided the models for their sermons and their practices of spiritual preparation. His pattern of retreating into hermitages as he travelled taught the crucial necessity of prayer for effective preaching. In fact, these out-of-the-way *retiros* were not an addition to other dwellings but were, in fact, the principal way that the friars sheltered in the early generations.

The hamlets and powerful citadels of Italy were not the only destinations Francis wanted to reach. The final commandment of Jesus, "Go, and teach all nations" echoed in his heart. Where was his preaching most needed? He tried to reach Morocco twice to preach to the Moslems. Once bad weather spoiled the voyage. His second try ended when he contracted a fever. He did, however, reach Spain where today countless pilgrims follow the Camino to the shrine of St. James in Compostella. When the time came to compose his written rule, he would be the first religious founder to include specific written instructions for such missionary ventures.

On a mountain in Tuscany he found a place to meditate and draw courage for future ventures. This mountain, called La Verna, was a gift from Count Orlando of Chiusi whose property it was. Here he and the brothers found themselves closer to heaven and distanced from the continual struggles they witnessed everywhere. In those hills and valleys of the Casentino, hermits and monks had cultivated the forests and a spirit of ascetic contemplation for centuries. Here was a place of perfect solitude to which he could return between exhausting travels.

By 1215 two new groups of preaching brothers were supporting the reforming work of Pope Innocent III. Francis's project was not the only response to the signs of the times. Dominic de Guzman was leading a brotherhood committed to combatting heresy. Dominic, an educated canon of St. Augustine, recognized the importance of meeting heretics on their own grounds of debate. He prepared his brothers with a systematic education in theology. The Archbishop of Toulouse brought him to Rome seeking papal approbation for this new "Order of Preachers." Dominic did not advance a new rule. He adopted the Rule of St. Augustine and the preachers flourished with the pope's blessing on their critical apostolate.

The Pope Calls a Council

Innocent III knew the time was ripe for consolidating his reforms. He convened a church council known as Lateran IV—its name taken from the papal cathedral in Rome. The assembly of bishops and cardinals would include the two leaders of new orders, Francis and Dominic. Convinced that he now had the right combination of dedicated clergy in these two orders, Innocent decreed that no new religious order or rule would be approved.

This decree would extend to women's monasteries and give rise to endless complications for Clare and her sisters.

Certain themes of renewed pastoral practice run through the legislation of this council. Its goals were adopted by Francis and his brotherhood. The teaching on the real presence of Christ in the Eucharist needed reinforcement. Legislation described details for caring for the reserved Eucharistic host, for the furnishings of altars and tabernacles. Priestly conduct had to be elevated and the manner of celebrating Mass demonstrate appropriate respect. Francis took this theme to heart and many of his writings and admonitions reflect his desire to foster this reverence for the gift of the Eucharist. He urged careful, mindful celebration of Mass by priests and reservation of the consecrated host in proper vessels. Later we will see that Clare and the sisters did their part by fashioning the linens needed to fulfill these requirements.

Mandatory education requirements were established to remedy the deplorable ignorance of the diocesan clergy. In their travels, the friars encountered much hostility to local clergy and were likely tempted to adopt such attitudes. This virulent disrespect was the product of peoples' frustration with priests who were ignorant, crude in manner and, in many instances, refusing compliance with the discipline of celibacy. More than once, Francis had to admonish his own brothers to show respect to priests regardless of their personal worthiness—or lack thereof. This tough stance reflected his intuitive understanding of the primary importance of maintaining unity in a church beset by the sinfulness of its members but redeemed by the holiness of its Head.

Changing Times

The brothers, too, now needed to be formed by proper instruction to ensure that their preaching was orthodox. Fortunately, they already had educated clerics in their midst. The most famous of these was Anthony of Padua—one of the friars' first official teachers. Francis sent Anthony a letter of approval. His singular warning was that the work of the classroom not suffocate the life of prayer. It was a plea for balance. It also hints at Francis's shrewd assessment of some university clerics who were more interested in displaying their own erudition than the radical truth of the Gospel.

Not long after the council, Francis returned to Assisi and arranged a meeting with Clare that included Bishop Guido II. They both wanted to keep Clare's sisterhood out of harm's way. She had no separate rule as she was considered to be living in the same spirit as the brothers whose rule had been approved in 1209. Would that accommodation stand? Francis had reason to think that Clare needed to demonstrate compliance with the new dictates of Rome. He asked her to accept a title of abbess. This was, of course, the usage of traditional Benedictine monasteries and it was a title of primacy and authority. She resisted. We can only guess at the negotiations that ensued. Finally, she did agree but she used the title sparingly throughout her life. This is one of very few instances of the two being out of sorts with each other, however briefly. Time would show that Francis's fears were justified and that winds of strict new laws for women were blowing northward from the Tiber.

The Brothers' Expansion

Pope Innocent survived only one more year after his council; his successor was Honorius III. In 1217 when the brothers convened at Portiuncula they numbered in the thousands. The stories of how they met and how the townspeople helped manage this medieval Woodstock became the stuff of legends. The fraternity was organized into provinces, each with its own minister in charge. Brothers were commissioned to Germany, Spain, France, Hungary, and Syria. It was understood that they would return at regular intervals to Assisi for these meetings with Francis. They were men on the move; their itinerancy was now established as key to their success.

Francis would aspire to go as far as the Holy Land. His famous voyage in 1219 took him into the camps of crusaders where the shock of their immoral behavior reduced him to despairing warnings of failure. With great care Francis constructed the plan to enter into the lands held by the Moslem armies under the command of Sultan Malek-al-Kamil. Once in the camp of the sultan, he conducted himself with such courage, humility, and chivalrous respect that the outcomes of the brave endeavor have become emblematic of Christian-Moslem dialogue to this day.

His long sojourn abroad had to be aborted when a friar arrived with news that the brotherhood was in danger of losing its way in his absence. Francis returned in 1220 and convened the brothers to deliberate in chapter. Recognizing that the exponential growth had taken the fraternity beyond his capacity for governance, he yielded his office of minister to Peter Catanii, a legally trained friar. Peter, however, died within a year and Francis then named Elias of Cortona, a trusted aide-de-camp, as the minister general. He also formally petitioned Pope Honorius for the services of Cardinal Hugolino as a protector for the burgeoning order.

Chapter Eight

ROME SPEAKS

*T*he work of Lateran IV was welcome news for those who worried about the success of the heretics and who were encouraged by the rise of the new mendicant preachers. Yet the need for major course correction, for establishing clear boundaries and norms, would inevitably create a chilling effect on new experiments in Christian living and preaching. The ground beneath Francis and Clare began to shift in this program of Church reform.

One of the important rulings was that no new religious orders would receive papal approval. The Poor Sisters were regarded as part of the "ordo" for which Francis had received approval in 1209. While there may not have been a sense of panic among the women, there was growing evidence that attention to form was becoming important in a new way. Clare was now being addressed as abbess in spite of her reluctance to use the title. Church dignitaries began to design legal structures to protect and control new expressions of female religious life.

Jacques de Vitry

One such dignitary was Bishop Jacques de Vitry. Part of his goal was to solicit papal approval for a group of religious women in his diocese of Liége. This particular group of beguines was founded by the saintly Marie d'Oignies. It was her fame that drew him from theology studies in Paris back to Belgium. Under her influence de Vitry became an Augustinian and eventually a preacher of enormous power and influence. He wrote of his delight in discovering new forms of religious life among women and men in the region of central Italy. He was seeking an audience with Innocent III who died before the bishop reached him. Jacques appears to be one of those leaders whose sensitivities to new expressions of holiness kept him open to voices that others ignored.

Cardinal Hugolino

Hugolino dei Conti di Segni, cardinal and bishop of Ostia and Vallera, was the ecclesiastical prince whose impact on the early Franciscans would be enormous. Honorius III—Innocent's successor—appointed Hugolino as delegate to the regions of Umbria, Tuscany, and Lombardy. His mandate was to develop uniform regulations for monasteries of women who did not already vow observance to the Benedictine or Cistercian rule. For these same monasteries, acceptance of a new rule, composed by Hugolino, would lead to incorporation into a new order directly supervised by papal authority. This text reads more like a constitution with its explicit details regarding the behavior and dress of the sisters and the construction of the cloister; however, the term *Rule* became the standard way of referring to it.

The cardinal's travels took him Florence, Lucca, Siena, Perugia, and, of course, to Assisi. By 1218, the new order was established. Clare and her sisters were exempted from total compliance with the Hugolinian Rule by reason of their formal relationship with Francis and the brothers. Managing a delicate détente with the cardinal, Clare sent her own sister, Agnes, to the monastery of Monticelli in Florence, which he had taken into his orbit, with the understanding that Monticelli would enjoy the exemption promised to San Damiano.

Within another two years, Honorius issued promulgations that designated these monasteries under the title *Order of Ladies of St. Damian of Assisi* and imposed the *Form and Mode of Living of the Poor Ladies* of Cardinal Hugolino. The confounding truth was that while the name of Clare's monastery was used to identify this new "order" of women's religious houses, Clare and her sisters were not legally part of it! Letters sent to the member monasteries were composed with San Damiano named as first in the list. Was this a subtle vote of confidence that Clare would eventually see the light and cross over to Hugolino's jurisdiction? It was, at the very least, a major propaganda *coup* and a brilliant bit of medieval branding and marketing. (It also would be the source of endless headaches for scholars trying to untangle this web of Poor Sisters and San Damiano houses up to the present day.)

Even a cursory reading of Hugolino's Rule reveals the stark contrast of spirit and letter with the spirit that characterized the first generations of sisters and brothers. It opens with a warning that "laxity and detestable sloth" may lead the sisters to neglect their promises. It commands that the sisters be fully enclosed for life. A new member is to be initiated into the "hard and austere realities" of religious life. Silence is kept at all times and speaking must be done with permission and all speaking requires that three persons be present. Iron grilles separate the sisters from those who wish to speak to them from the outside. Doors are secured with iron bars, strong beams, door panels and keys.

Complex instructions for days of fasting include some allowance of mitigation for the sick. The habit is described in great detail and includes two tunics, a mantel, a hair shirt, scapulars of woven cloth—which appear to be regarded as having special religious significance. Beds are to be planks of wood. No one enters the monastery without papal permission, which can be granted by the cardinal protector. Provision is made for a chaplain to offer Mass and an official visitator who may regularly evaluate the spirit of the monastery in person. Finally, workmen may enter—accompanied of course—to provide such services as digging a grave. Also, a doctor could enter to treat the sisters.

While the exemption that was granted to the poor sisters allowed for continued refusal of ownership of any property and close reliance upon Francis and the brothers, the growing insistence upon such traditional monastic disciplines would influence the observances of San Damiano over time. When those accommodations to papal direction took place, however, the unique spirit of Clare and the sisters would infuse the regulations with a spirit of charitable and prudential wisdom.

Cardinal Protector and Pope
During this time Francis was pursuing his call to preach to the crusading armies and the Moslem enemies of Christendom. In Holy Week of 1220, the cardinal made a personal visit to Clare and her sisters. Naturally he hoped by this pastoral outreach to convince her to finally accept the Rule and full membership in his new order which, conveniently, bore the name of her monastery. She declined and repeated her conviction that the vocation she shared with Francis and its Gospel foundation were the rules by which she had vowed to live.

Following this visit, Hugolino sent a letter overflowing with personal admiration and humble gratitude for the time spent with the abbess of penitents and poor sisters. He laments being "separated from your holy conversation" and finding himself "desolate by your absence from me." He tells her that he is convinced that his sins can only be forgiven if "your prayers and tears obtain for me pardon for my sins." He goes on. "I entrust my soul and commend my spirit to you, just as Jesus on the Cross commended His spirit to His Father...." He closes with the promise that he "will seize the first opportunity in my desire to see you and your sisters." To this he adds special greetings for Agnes who presides over his foundation in Florence. Knowing the tension between them, we may wonder at the apparent emotional overflow of this message. It appears that Hugolino was deeply interested in and inspired by the phenomenon of holy women whose ascetical and mystical lives were powerful forces for renewal of the church. He had, in fact, requested that Jacques de Vitry supply him with a relic of Marie d'Oignies, a relic he always carried on his person.

Perhaps it was this combination of administrative talent with a hunger for authentic Christian holiness that prompted Francis to choose Hugolino as the man who could best support the sisters and the whole of his fraternity as well. This critical step preceded an emergency chapter in which Francis relinquished the title of minister and named Peter Catanii in his stead. Francis's unerring intuition moved him to renounce his office while securing a strong papal oversight for the friars. In this way he hoped to stabilize a brotherhood that was growing so quickly that its founding charism was endangered.

Though respected by both Clare and Francis, Hugolino none-theless was unable to fully endorse the radical nature of their desire to live the Gospel in literal and comprehensive fashion. Their willingness to embrace extremes of renunciation rubbed against his sense of duty to the centralizing programs of the Roman curia. He was, for all of that, to serve as a key player throughout the lifetime of Francis and, later as pope, the life of Clare as well.

Chapter Nine

Weaving a Way of Life

These years were full of work, struggle, sickness, hardship, and joyous events and encounters. New monasteries grew in number. The rules of cloister specifically permitted an abbess to leave her monastery to officiate at the founding of a "daughter house." Did Clare exercise this option? Only a few monasteries took their pattern directly from that of Clare and her sisters in Assisi. Her direct influence would have played a role in their establishment. Many others were part of the broader consortium of monasteries that depended upon the legislation of Hugolino and the tidal wave of documents by which Roman offices monitored the sisters. Preservation of the original intentions she shared with Francis occupied her days. They were of one mind in holding to this standard. The simple Gospel program that each sister accepted when she joined the group must be renewed over and over. Clare accomplished this by a steady stream of instruction. This teaching helped all—the youngest to the elders—to preserve a difficult commitment. The teaching also urged a spirit of joyful identification with the trials of Jesus who was himself "a man of suffering, accustomed to infirmity" (Isaiah 53:3).

The rhythms of prayer marked the days and the seasons. From the font of the Divine Office Clare and her sisters drew the wealth of the Psalter and other Scriptures, the writings of the Church fathers, the lyrics of ancient hymns. This ancient form of prayer required that the sisters gather throughout the day and night. These "hours" bore the names Matins, Lauds, Prime, Tierce, Sext, None, Vespers, Compline. The seasons of Advent, Christmas, Lent, Easter, and Pentecost recurred each year, bringing a deepening immersion in the life of Jesus and the liturgical cycle of feasts and fasts. The unique Office of the Passion, composed by Francis, added a continual focus on the sufferings of Jesus, sufferings that were redeemed by the ultimate victory willed by God, the Most High King. The stories of saints and martyrs filled minds and hearts with examples of courage and devotion. Special affection was accorded the memory of great women of earlier times: Agnes and Cecilia of Rome, Catherine of Alexandria, Mary Magdalene, and, of course, the Mother of Christ and Queen of Virgins.

The Work of their Hands

It was important to maintain health and vigor among the sisters. The fasting practices, the frequent outbreaks of various contagions, the close quarters of the place, made for a constant pattern of sickness among them. The healing charism Clare possessed was part of a larger pattern of medical assistance given regularly by the women of San Damiano. Increasing the rules of enclosure over time created some difficulty for the sisters in managing their own economic needs. Yet, they had a way to provide a valuable service to churches in the region. They produced the linens

needed to celebrate Mass and for the Eucharistic host and rel-
ics. The Lateran Council had promulgated specific decrees that
dictated the use of clean linens and worthy receptacles. Francis
was an eager publicist for these reforms. That the ladies of San
Damiano would possess the necessary skill and artistry was a
given. Women were tutored in such skills in noble families. For
the women who came from the *minores*, work in some aspect of
cloth trade was a way of life. To be sure, a community of women
with this combination of talents might clearly support itself by
creating such a cottage industry. So it is that we read about Clare
spinning even in later years when she was confined to her bed.
The cloth that her spinning created was then fashioned by the
sisters into the needed forms. They would then be organized
and placed in boxes. Some of these were covered in silk. Then,
having been blessed by the bishop, they were delivered to all of
the parishes of the region. The details of this industrious activity
were recalled when the sisters testified at the investigation after
Clare's death.

One detail of that testimony is worth some comment. Clare
and the sisters covered boxes in silk. No more is said about the
existence of such a fabric in their monastery. Silk was the most
precious of materials and normally its possession was the prerogative of the wealthy classes. Did the Poor Sisters fashion the
silk themselves? Was it procured from other women's businesses?
The silk trade was controlled by women throughout Europe.
Access to silk was the prerogative of the rich. The possibility
that the sisters either made or could barter for silk suggests that
theirs was a sophisticated production. They stood at the head of
a long line of nuns whose days would be occupied with creating

and caring for the vessels, vestments, and materials needed for the sacred liturgy.

Probably the most frequent visitors came needing help and prayers. The sisters were sought out when need arose in Assisi and nearby towns. The ordinary remedies and skills of more than one sister would be in constant demand. The monastery's origins as a hospice revived as friars and others came there for healing and restoration. While we will look closely at the healing ministry of Clare later, it is enough to say that the reputation of San Damiano was a magnet for those in need. From serious conditions of body and soul to the normal childhood emergency—like the small boy with a stone stuck in his nose—Clare and the sisters were a "go to" font of expert help. Sometimes the need was for prayer, advice, and admonition. A marriage in trouble, a battle threatened, a family quarrel to solve—all petitions would find wise counsel and ardent prayer offered generously.

Official episcopal visits to San Damiano were, to be sure, rare but most memorable. Bishop Guido, who had done so much to support the early foundation, died and his successor bore the same name, Guido II. He came with Francis and admonished Clare to end her dangerous fasting. He may have visited to bless the sacred linens the women created or to celebrate specific events and feasts. We know of the Easter sojourn of Cardinal Hugolino. This was only one of many visits he would have made as the protector of the sisters. (Later he would be elected pope and return following the canonization of Francis.) While Francis was gone to Egypt, did the interim ministers seek Clare's advice and prayer? Specially appointed visitors from both the Cistercians and the friars were obliged to make formal evaluations. They celebrated Mass and preached to the sisters on many occasions. Clare was able to maintain written communications with other monasteries to which she had sent sisters. The friars would have been the most likely postal service. Surely the arrival of brothers bearing news or letters from any of these sister foundations would have marked a red-letter day.

.

Chapter Ten

A SEAL UPON THE HEART

The expedition of Francis and his companion, Brother Illuminato, to the camp of Sultan Malek-al-Kamil in 1219 has become a touchstone for today's Christian project of dialogue with Islam. But when Francis returned to his homeland in the summer of 1220 he was burdened by a sense of failure. He had not convinced the sultan of the truth of Christian faith; the carnage of the crusade continued. In addition, Francis was alarmed by the news that, in his absence, the directives that guided the brothers were being set aside by his appointed deputies. The reality that greeted him upon his return confirmed his worst fears. The constantly growing fraternity was in crisis stemming from the difficulty of establishing uniform compliance with Francis's instructions. Trusted followers must now take up his administrative duties while Francis set about composing a "regula"—a rule—that would secure his vision for the brotherhood.

This was not an easy decision. Francis clung to the belief that the Gospel itself was the primary rule of the brothers. It was the bottomless well of inspiration that fashioned the early years and served as the manual for decision-making when they were few in number. Yet he had to respond to increasing demands from the brothers for clarity about the nature of their obligations. Their conscientious legal concerns were substantial. If, by vow, they were responsible for obedience to the whole of the Gospel, how could they avoid sinning, failing in their duty? Such perfection was too much to ask. What was the precise nature of their obligation? Now he was faced with the ultimate irony of his convictions. His belief that each brother came through the inspiration of the Holy Spirit now required that he listen and obey that communal voice even if it thrust a sword into his heart.

The Seal of the Pope

Clare had no rule for her own community beyond the simple *Form of Life* Francis provided at the beginning. She and her sisters lived by organizational osmosis. The manner of life of the friars was the form of their own and they had learned to translate those elements to suit their feminine milieu. She would be alert to the significant change taking place in the brotherhood since her own patterns of teaching and living were intimately linked to theirs.

By 1221, Francis composed a Rule that he submitted to Honorius III for approval. It was a collection of disparate forms drawn from the lived experiences of the brothers. The central commitment to live the form of the holy Gospel was there. Instructions about how to receive new members, how to correct failures, and what type of work could be done—these and other matters of good order were clarified. The lengthy document also included exhortations about how the brothers should preach. There were lyrical passages of prayer. Francis hoped to preserve his experience of penitential holiness and the evangelical mission which he included in these expansive meditations. Rome, however, was not to be moved by poetry or passionate appeals. What was required was a text that was crystal clear about the things that were essential elements of membership. Francis's personal example and admonitions no longer sufficed to unify discipline. His closest advisors and church superiors prevailed, and Francis went back to the drawing board.

Clare might well have sympathized as Francis set about writing these texts. That pontifical seal was more important to him than a personal triumph of getting his way with words. He knew that the protection of his order depended upon this highest authorization. For years following Francis's death, Clare continued in friendship with his closest companions. These were the friars who had the most intimate knowledge of his struggles in that protracted debate between the brothers and the church authorities. A time would come when she would demonstrate her conviction that the quest for papal approval was worth the sacrifice it entailed.

The Seal of Christ

Having finally secured the pope's approval in November of 1223, Francis made his way to the Rieti Valley. There, with Christmas approaching, he visited Greccio where his early preaching had found a ready audience. The task of the Rule settled, he returned to his life's work of making Jesus present to the people. This was the motive for his recreation of the Christmas event during midnight Mass in that village. With the assistance of local friends and a carefully designed liturgical innovation, he gifted the people with a recreation of the scene of the Nativity in a cave in Bethlehem. The cave of the nearby mountainside became the backdrop. Mass was celebrated there in the midst of animals and other figures to represent the Gospel story. It electrified the people and created an indelible memory destined to give rise to an enduring custom—the *praesepio*—the Christmas crib.

Nine months after the joyful Greccio celebration, Francis withdrew to La Verna filled with doubt and sorrow. His spirit was in torment. Only his secretary, Leo, was permitted to remain near him. There, in the September days of 1224, Francis received the wounds of Christ printed into his body during a mystical experience of the Crucified Love. The sisters would later realize that at this very time, Clare became seriously ill and never fully recovered her former strength.

Six months passed. Francis came to San Damiano for care. His companions were sworn to secrecy about the miraculous vision of Christ, but the fact of the wounds and the resulting pain were adding to his rapid physical decline. For all of the torment Clare now witnessed, she had the joy of being able to serve him with all of her skill. Not only was she able to see to the medicinal help he needed, but she provided special slippers to protect his feet from the excruciating pain of the wounds. Clare had spent years in adoration before the Cross that had called him from sin. Who could better understand what was transpiring? This fact of stigmatization was totally new in Christian experience. These confidential companions struggled to comprehend it and to trust the evidence of their own eyes. Only with the formal notice of Francis's death was the miracle made public. It would, to be sure, be controversial through the ages. For Clare, controversy was unimaginable. She bathed and dressed those wounds barely daring to breath. She saw—as few would ever see—what a poet would later call Francis's "Veronica-veil of flesh." His early promise to lead her to intimacy with Jesus was fulfilled as she beheld the incarnate icon of the Crucified Son of God.

Out of that pain and darkness, Francis's spirit rose up in thanksgiving and praise as he composed his immortal *Canticle of the Sun*. This poem would forever be associated with San Damiano. Here their shared vocation flowered in a poem that calls upon all of creation to join in a cosmic chorus of gratitude for life and for the very earth that sustains it. Francis wrote in the Umbrian dialect and a melody accompanied the words. The brothers could sing it as a way of calling people to prayer. Meaning it to be used in real cities with real problems, Francis soon added verses that also made it a call to reconciliation with one's enemies, even with the ultimate enemy, Death.

When Francis seeks to describe the stars of night, he uses the word clarite. He calls the stars *"clarite, pretiose et belle"*— clear, precious, beautiful. *Clarite* is a new word—bridging the gap between Latin and the Umbrian dialect of Italian. Do the moments of her loving help become the "clear stars" in the night of his increasing pain and weakness? Does the beauty of her fidelity to Christ and her sisters ease his fears for the future? Does this final time of daily encounter assure him that none have been more faithful to the precious dream of an evangelical renaissance than the Lady Clare?

Chapter Eleven

COMPANIONS SIGNED BY THE CROSS

This account of the final sojourn of Francis at San Damiano shows the continuing role of Clare as he endured mental and bodily torment. It was a unique episode that allowed her to care for his critical physical needs. She surely suffered while witnessing his intractable pain. Yet, she would have rejoiced in being a presence during these days and nights—a presence of competent nursing care and consummate spiritual mutuality. This final encounter was unique and begs the question of how their relationship grew over time. What opportunities did they have to share the mysteries of divine inspiration, the ups and downs of forming new communities, the threats from within and without to their project? How often did they actually spend time in each other's presence?

A small number of actual examples come from the sources we have. Their relationship spans fifteen years from the first encounters in 1211 to the death of Francis in 1226. While Francis's example and teaching guided Clare's every undertaking, we have many blanks to fill in as we trace the evolution of their friendship. We can single out those instances we do know about.

At the start, we know that a series of secret meetings took place between the two and their prudently assigned companions.

The culmination of Clare's investiture and subsequent transfers to San Paolo, Sant'Angelo and San Damiano involved Francis directly. It appears that these first years of Clare's participation were ones in which they had the most frequent contact. We know that during those years he was inspired by the courage with which she and the early sisters took on the challenges inherent in founding San Damiano. That experience grounded his continuing admiration and confidence in her.

As time passed certain visits left a notable impression and were recorded. Here are the examples we do have.

At one point Francis brought a group of five women as candidates for the sisters' community. (It appears that even when he was not in frequent personal communication with the Poor Sisters, he kept them in mind.) Clare immediately sensed that one of these candidates would not be a suitable member and told Francis so. He, however, urged her to reconsider. She relented but in the end her intuition proved right and the woman departed. The most interesting aspect of this incident is the revelation that Clare demonstrated her independence of judgment in relation to her teacher just as she had in the matter of her being named as abbess. She did not treat Francis as a demigod whose word was magic. It is interesting to speculate how often this might have been the nature of their conversations even though we only have these two examples.

Francis recognized Clare's gift for healing. He sent sick persons to the monastery. A notable instance was the case of Brother Stephen. This friar was in mental torment and Francis personally brought him there. Clare prayed for his healing and had him sleep in that place of prayer. He woke restored and returned to his fraternity.

Two of their meetings had legal matters as the topic. We have seen that Francis came to San Damiano to convince her to accept the title of abbess. In another such visit—this one also included Bishop Guido II—he implored her to stop her radical fasting and take measures to protect her health. That he had to exercise such strong oversight indicates another ironic aspect of their relationship. Clare's independence led to actions that others judged to be dangerous. Francis was forced to intervene and did so with all possible urgency.

In later years Francis intentionally curtailed his visits. Elias, who was clearly attuned to Clare's anxieties, urged him on multiple occasions to visit San Damiano. Francis's response to these entreaties deserves our attention. Francis is said to have replied:

> Don't imagine, dear brothers, that I don't love them fully. For if it were a crime to cherish them in Christ, wouldn't it be even worse to have joined them to Christ? Not calling them would not have been harmful, but not to care for them after calling them would be the height of cruelty. But I am giving you an example, that as I do, so should you also do." (2 Celano CLVI)

Francis was grappling with the tension of providing example in a matter of important discipline—the issue of proper relationships between men and women obligated to lives of chastity. No doubt, scandalous lapses among the brothers combined with episcopal pressures were forcing Francis to set a high bar for himself and the others. Clare and her sisters had to bear the brunt of this change in his demeanor. Finally, Francis relented and went to the monastery. The form of his sermon, however, was an about face. Instead of words of instruction or consolation he performed a penitential ritual. Seated on the ground, he sprinkled his head with ashes while reciting the Miserere (Psalm 51). Was he signaling that his earlier familiarity had to yield to monastic protocol? Had something transpired that would be readily understood by Clare and her sisters when he performed this mime? Was it, after all, a consummate expression of trust that his sisters would understand that no words of his were adequate to what was needed in that season?

Dangerous Memories

In a category by itself is the account in the fifteenth chapter of the *Fioretti*. It describes a shared meal that Francis arranged for Clare at the Portiuncula. The narrative portrays him as eager to allow such a reunion in the place where she first entered into their company. She and her companion arrive and their conversation centers on the gifts of grace which both have received. The ardor of this exchange is so intense that the villagers nearby believe they see flames enveloping the small church. They rush to save the place only to find Francis, Clare, and companions fully caught up in this divine discourse and aflame with God's love.

Since this account comes from a set of stories written long after both were dead, it is often treated as a mere folktale. Yet, its telling indicates that years after they lived, this spirit of a profound mutual delight in God's gifts was fondly remembered. It was the heart of a friendship of grace. It was a story worth saving.

Our final evidence for the depth of relationship between the two comes from the witness for Clare's canonization, Sr. Filippa.

She alone relates a remarkable dream that Clare shared with her. Here is the description:

> Lady Clare also related how once, in a vision, it seemed to her she brought a bowl of hot water to Saint Francis, along with a towel for drying his hands. She was climbing a very high stairway, but was going very quickly, almost as though she were going on level ground. When she reached Saint Francis the saint bared his breast and said to the Lady Clare: "Come, take, and drink." After she had sucked from it, the saint admonished her to imbibe once again. After she did so what she had tasted was so sweet and delightful she could in no way describe it. After she had imbibed, the nipple or opening of the breast from which the milk comes remained between the lips of blessed Clare. After she took what remained in her mouth in her hands, it seemed to her it was gold so clear and bright everything was seen in it as in a mirror. (Process, III:29)

More than one Franciscan scholar has approached this text with understandable hesitation. Our post-Freudian mentality assigns all sort of meanings that would have astounded Clare. It is obvious that such a dream reflects a powerful bond, one that is as primal as that of a nursing mother and her child. She seeks to provide some refreshment or help to Francis. Her pace is swift, and her ascent is without effort. The encounter that results is stunning to modern eyes. He nurses her with a sweet milk that fills her with delight. When this mystical nursing ends, she holds a golden mirror that is the remnant of their intimate embrace. In that mirror she sees all goodness.

What could explain this extraordinary dream and its sensual images? It turns out that monastic leaders of the period did use the image of a nursing mother as a symbol for how an abbot should relate to the ones in his charge. No less a figure than Bernard of Clairvaux urged his abbots: "Learn that you must be mothers to those in your care...expose your breasts, let your bosoms expand with milk." The notion of a maternal stance toward his followers was part of Francis's mindset and appears in his writing for the friars. It was also a time when scholars and abbots described Jesus as a mother to his children.

Here, for the woman to whom he promised "care and solicitude," he is symbolized in this intimate maternal act. However often or seldom Francis was physically accessible to Clare and her sisters, there can be no doubt that the spiritual bonds that united them defy easy description. The utopian dream of our return to the Garden of Eden, to walk in the cool shades of evening as male and female friends of the Creator—this is the hope that lives in these remarkable stories.

Writings in Place of Visits

Francis placed great importance on sending a written text when he could not be present in person or when he wanted to underscore the importance of his message. Earlier we spoke of the written "Form of Life," which he provided so that Clare would have evidence of his intentions about her community. That message would play a central role when she wrote her own Rule and Life. It reads: "Because by divine inspiration you have made yourselves daughters and handmaids of the most High, most exalted King, the heavenly Father, and have taken the Holy Spirit as your spouse, choosing to live according to the perfection of the holy Gospel, I resolve and promise for myself and for my brothers always to have the same loving care and special solicitude for you as for them."

Here are the other important texts he provided.

The "Last Will" for Clare and her sisters is known to us because it, too, is incorporated into her Rule. It appears to have been a final exhortation to stay the course:

> I, little brother Francis, wish to follow the life and poverty of our most high Lord Jesus Christ and of his most holy Mother and to persevere in this until the end; and I ask you, my Ladies, and I give you my advice that you live always in this most holy life and poverty. And keep careful watch that you never depart from this by reason of the teaching or advice of anyone." (*Form of Life* XII, 7-9)

Two really important writings were transmitted while he stayed at San Damiano for medical help. At the time of his confinement there, he wrote a lovely short greeting called "The Canticle of Exhortation to St. Clare and her Sisters."

Since the title "Canticle" is now used, it appears that it may have been intended to be sung—much as a troubadour would sing to praise the ladies of a royal court. Like the better known Canticle of the Creatures, it is written in the Umbrian dialect and is sometimes referred to by its first word, the *Audite*.

> Listen, little poor ones, called by the Lord, who have come together from many parts and provinces. Live always in truth that you may die in obedience. Do not look at the life outside, for that of the Spirit is better. I beg you through great love, to use with discretion the alms which the Lord gives you.

Those who are weighed down by sickness and the others who are wearied because of them, all of you: bear it in peace. For you will sell this fatigue at a very high price and each one [of you] will be crowned queen in heaven with the Virgin Mary. (*Canticle of Exhortation*, 1-6)

Finally, Francis wrote his immortal *Canticle of the Creatures* while in Clare's care at San Damiano. The incredible power and poetry of this song has long fascinated all who read, study, or sing it. One word in that poem, written in Umbrian dialect, and written during a time of daily nursing by Clare, catches the eye. It is the word *clarite*. "Praised be you, my Lord, through Sister Moon and the stars, in heaven you formed them clear and precious and beautiful" (Canticle, 5). This is the adjective for the stars. They are "*clarite et pretiose et belle*,"—clear, precious, beautiful. In the long dark time of his illness, was it Clare who was this "*pretiose, belle, clarite*" companion whose light helped him endure encroaching blindness and searing pain? She had been—and would remain—the North Star for all who wanted to follow his way.

Chapter Twelve

THE DEATH OF FRANCIS

*A*fter the sojourn at San Damiano, Elias organized multiple trips to find treatments for Francis. Finally, they returned—with an armed escort—to the house of Assisi's bishop. With death drawing ever closer, he asked to be taken to his beloved Santa Maria degli Angeli, the Portiuncula. Every person in the region was aware of the Poverello's impending death. Already hailed as a saint, he would bestow a lasting benefit to the place where he died and was buried. The politics of a saint's cult and the power of a holy shrine was no small matter to a medieval town. The burial place of *this* saint was destined to become a shrine of importance—a magnet for pilgrims who brought not only penitence and prayers, but pocketbooks as well. The fear of him being carried off as a trophy to Perugia or another rival commune was too much to bear. Security guards were at the ready to prevent such sabotage. The *podestá* (mayor) and bishop had already agreed upon post-mortem protocols. The vigil in the valley was mirrored in every household in the city. The commune was holding its collective breath.

Clare was not to see him again. Her ardent hope for yet one more visit went unfulfilled. He had, however, sent the final "testament" that she would cherish and insert into her own Rule decades later. Years after his death, friars would recall that Francis, having received her entreaty, sent word to her to *"put aside her grief and sorrow over not being able to see me now."*

Brothers hovered around him providing whatever care they could; his friend and benefactor, Lady Jacoba Settisoli, arrived from Rome with material for his burial shroud, candles for the services, and most famously, the almond cookies that he enjoyed during visits to her palazzo in Rome. Finally, that wracked and ravaged body was to be given a bit of human comfort. (And generations of lesser mortals would be relieved to learn that he was, at the last, simply human—and hungry for comfort food.)

The friar messengers were busy. Reports were required in the city, in the palace of the bishop, and in the cloister of San Damiano. Clare kept vigil in grief-laden prayer. News of his words, his visitors, the arrival of Lady Jacoba, his final Gospel rituals reached her as the hours crawled by. On October third, as the sun slid behind the mountains to the west, the larks spun a cloud of song into the apricot sky. Francis breathed his last.

It is not too much to imagine that she had no need of a messenger that night.

The Funeral

The next day a cortege bringing the body of Francis for burial in the church of San Giorgio came to the monastery. There, Clare and her sisters were able to give voice to their grief. Later Francis's first biographer, Thomas of Celano, would describe the women's unrestrained laments. A most poignant record of that hour is found in the Basilica of St. Francis in the fresco of Giotto. The artist depicted the sisters, their faces taut with grief. Sadly for us, damages to this fresco have erased the face of Clare. Only by studying the expressions of the crowd of mourners, the friars bearing the body, and the sisters who stand behind her can we imagine what they see. Their vision encompasses both the bier carrying Francis's lifeless body and the face of Clare. The sight moves them deeply and doubles their own sense of loss. Her bereavement could hardly be equaled since for her, as for her sisters, Francis was "after God, her only consolation." Now she must face an abyss of solitude in the quest for Gospel perfection. Thomas of Celano etches an indelible image: "Once he was taken away, the door that never again will suffer such pain, was closed on them" (*First Life of St. Francis*, Part II, Chapter X, 27).

Indeed, the door closed on an experience of shared charisms that would never be rivalled. The time of grief did not reduce Clare to a shadowy survivor of the "good old days." Rather, the immediate fires of loss and increased episcopal pressure to abandon their original plan only fortified her determination to stay the course. She would be the "lampstand to enlighten all in the house" of Francis. If the first half of her life had been spent in constructing the path with him, the second would be spent insisting on its trustworthiness as the penitent pilgrim's road. She will live to enflesh the prophetic declaration:

> I will stand at my guard post, and station myself upon the rampart, and keep watch to see what he will say to me, and what answer he will give to my complaint. Then the Lord answered me and said: Write down the vision clearly upon the tablets, so that one can read it readily. For the vision still has its time, presses on to fulfillment, and will not disappoint; if it delays wait for it, it will surely come, and it will not be late. (Habakkuk 2:1-3)

Intermission

....

*F*rancis died in 1226. Clare died in 1253. She survived his death by twenty-seven years. This fact demands attention. It is this fact that underscores the magnitude of her place among the early generations of the Franciscan movement. Time and a great deal of collaboration among experts offers us the material we need. Gradually we are beginning to gauge correctly the importance of her actions, her role as the new leader not only among women but among friars seeking integral evolution of their order as well. The effort to tell the story of these years yields a whole new appreciation of who she would become within her lifetime. It is in the accurate and increasingly revelatory history of this woman that the radical equality of Franciscan charisms—those of women as well as those of men—is validated.

Perhaps a key can be found in the brilliant final scene of Lin-Manuel Miranda's *Hamilton*. The fateful shot that ended Hamilton's life closes what seems to be the last act. Or does it? Another scene follows. His wife, Eliza, is center stage. She ponders the question of who will tell his story. Eliza sings of her continuing quest to make sure that Hamilton's real story will be told. She reads the thousands of pages of his writings; she speaks out against slavery; she raises funds for the Washington Monument; she creates New York City's first private orphanage. She, in other words, keeps the promise made by Hamilton and the founders for their young nation. Eliza's spirit of living into the vision of the Founders is a modern vantage point for our reading of the next chapters of Clare's biography. Clare would emerge from the prison of grief to spend the years living each day to bring new incarnations of the Gospel to her sisters, her brothers, her city. Centuries later, Eliza Hamilton exhibits that same tenacity. Making sure the right version of the story gets told is not for the faint of heart.

Trying to map the chronology of those twenty-seven years yields nuggets of gold—the great anecdotes, new friendships, and actual events—as well as long stretches of little to report. The mapmaker realizes that there are certain patterns and themes that constantly recur. A simple date-by-date narrative works but it runs the risk of a certain tedium. After all, too many days with too little content will hardly keep one's pulse elevated or the bedtime reader from nodding off. For that reason we will dedicate the following chapters to these themes: her healing charism, her prayer, her penitential practices, her teaching and writing. These four strands are found throughout the story. In this way we hope to see the gifts that increased her fame and grounded her soul.

Once we have completed that attempt, we will return to the calendar of events of her final years.

II

Chapter Thirteen

HOLDING FAST TO THE LIFE

*I*t would not take long after the death of Francis for the heavy intervention of church authority to make itself felt in the monastery of Clare. From Rome, news of continued efforts to organize women's monasteries into a unified system of observance continued. Cardinal Hugolino was elected pope and took the name Gregory IX. The following year all was ready for the canonization of Francis. This event brought Gregory back to Assisi where he had spent so much time as Cardinal Protector. The joy and solemnity of the ceremonies completed, the pope made his way to San Damiano. Now he could urge Clare to accept *his* rule, *his* program. Knowing that she was adamant about the need to refrain from financial security, he offered to absolve her from the vow she had made to maintain such strict poverty. To this offer, she made the response that has echoed over the centuries: "Holy Father, I will never in any way wish to be absolved from the following of Christ" (*Legend of Clare*, 14 [17]).

Cardinal Protector

Shortly after this encounter, Gregory entrusted the role of Cardinal Protector to his nephew, Rainaldo. Rainaldo had accompanied his uncle, then Cardinal Hugolino, to meet the women religious of central Italy. Thus, he had the advantage of specialized expertise. Gregory also named Brother Philip as visitator for the sisters. Clare knew that her best course of action would be to meet papal power in a spirit of compromise. She accepted much of the legislation for her sisters but with the *proviso* that she and her sisters would never be ordered to accept the possession of property. The official document of this agreement was delivered to San Damiano in 1228. It is known by the title of "The Privilege of Poverty." After this hard-won concession, Gregory's communication with the Abbess of San Damiano faded.

In addition to her vigilance about property, Clare was determined to maintain the all-important direct connection to the friars who were now known by their approved title of Friars Minor or "lesser brothers." This was a matter of major importance even though Francis was no longer the chief mediator of that relationship. The friars, on their part, were also facing major difficulties with keeping the spirit and letter of their demanding Rule. In 1230 a group of four highly educated brothers went to Rome to present these difficulties to the pope. Among the problems in need of a pontifical solution was the obligation of providing for the spiritual care of the women's monasteries. Friars who could move throughout Europe and beyond to preach did not always appreciate being assigned to a monastery that kept them from more exciting assignments. Gregory decreed that the friars would not enter any monasteries for such pastoral service. Here was another blow to the entire *zeitgeist* of San Damiano. Clare's response was unequivocal. Knowing that this decision would cut to the heart the mutual commitments she and Francis made, she went on a hunger strike. Again, her words echo: "Let him now take away from us all the brothers since he has taken away those who provide us with the food that is vital" (LegCl 37). At once she sent the assisting brothers back to the minister, refusing to have them beg for bread from Assisi's ovens, when they could not give the spiritual bread of preaching and sacraments. News of her provocative response reached the Pope Gregory. Alarmed by the ferocity of her stance, he issued an exemption for San Damiano. He directed the successor of Francis, Minister General John Parenti, to see to the spiritual as well as physical needs of San Damiano.

Not long after, John Parenti was succeeded by Brother Elias, who was charged with the task of building a shrine worthy of the recently canonized saint. While the reputation of Elias has suffered for centuries because of this expensive undertaking (and his later skirmishes with papal authority) it is clear that Clare maintained the highest trust in him. The record indicates that he managed to protect San Damiano from additional interventions of church officials and took the work of maintaining the original compact of sisters and brothers seriously.

Grief over the loss of Francis was now compounded by the sadness of finding herself bound to an endless cycle of struggles to preserve their shared ideals. The community of sisters needed to move through evolutionary stages of formalizing their manner of life. In agreement with prescriptions of church law the sisters would demonstrate good faith and prudent discernment in observing common norms for religious women at the time.

Enclosure—the Cloister

Enclosure or cloister for nuns and religious women was important. It functioned on several levels. The first was simple physical security needed to protect women living together and removed from the safety of being domiciled with father or husband. Layers of meaning remain. It insured avoidance of secular pursuits and distractions in order to perfect a life of prayer. The observance of the penitential aspects of living in strict enclosure was interpreted as spiritual identification with Jesus in his sufferings and death. In fact, a spirituality of identification with the dying and buried Jesus was taken to extremes in some treatises on the importance of living cloistered and "dead to the world." This manner of life, focused on continual prayer and penance, had the social significance of providing a type of spiritual "insurance policy" for royal families, the people of a region, and the rulers of church and state. The prayers of the nuns were a surrogate offering meant to bring God's help to those who did not trust their own prayers or the wideness of divine mercy.

Undergirding all these layers was the profound cultural assumption—codified in Roman law—of the duty for the *paterfamilias* to make provision for the women of his kinship and to protect their chastity. While this shared understanding of the patriarch's responsibility was pervasive, it did not mean that in every instance the women who founded monastic or communitarian forms had no room for experimentation. In some monasteries, enclosure was very rigid. Others adopted a "modified" enclosure with allowances that provided flexibility to meet physical need or participate in ecclesiastical business. Finally, the symbolism of enclosure had its own power. Few could ignore the clear message that a woman, once taken into such a community, was truly off limits to familial marriage schemes, sexual liaisons, engagement in the temporal affairs of family, city, or diocese. In other words, the physical barriers communicated a vocational reality that demanded respectful compliance from those on the outside.

When Clare and her sisters studied the Rule of Hugolino they found a stringent code. We can recall key prescriptions of this legislation first given by Cardinal Hugolino—now Pope Gregory IX. Doors would be locked to visitors and fortified with "strong beams and iron bars." Admission was gained only through special circumstances—care of the sick, burial of the deceased, or work requiring male laborers. The areas where an outsider might speak to a sister were covered with iron grates. Even the most mundane conversation would take place in the presence of two other sisters. The dress was the formal attire of monastic nuns with specific instructions on the manner in which the habit would be made and worn. Fasting was semi-permanent with several periods of the year in which bread and water fasts were observed. The sisters were obliged to keep silence—to refrain from ordinary conversation—for many periods of each day. Perhaps the singular exception to this austere regimen was the instruction on the care of the sick where some relaxation in the fasting and silence was permitted.

Many a modern reader will find it difficult—if not impossible—to imagine living under such restrictions. That said, it is important to take Clare at her word here as in other matters. Nowhere does she register objection to having enclosure or cloister observed at San Damiano. What is clear is that Clare described its obligations in her own style and made prudent allowances for common sense and necessity. Her voice spoke in a register markedly different from that of Hugolino-Gregory IX. That unique voice would not remain confined to her monastery.

Other women asked for her guidance and sought formal identification with San Damiano. Not mistaking the papal Order of San Damiano for the original Franciscan sisterhood of Clare, these women formed a small circle of adherence to poverty and room for the accompaniment of the friars. The circle, however, was destined to be enlarged and empowered by the emergence of one of the most remarkable of Clare's soul sisters, Agnes of Prague.

Chapter Fourteen

AGNES OF PRAGUE

Seven years after Francis's death, a group of friars took up residence in Prague, seat of the Premysl dynasty. The Bohemian crown princess, Agnes, expended her energies and her considerable wealth in creating foundations for the friars and the Poor Sisters. A group of Clare's sisters from Trent arrived in 1233 and almost at once eleven Bohemian women entered the new monastery. One year later the princess herself entered the monastery with the blessing of her brother, King Wenceslaus, and the instruction of Pope Gregory IX that she be installed as the abbess. With this royal foundation rising, a remarkable correspondence between the Abbess of Penitents and the princess-turned-abbess began.

The litany of royal marriage proposals for Agnes was long and labyrinthine. Promises of her hand in marriage began when she was a small child. They continued through a progression of broken promises by royal suitors, political intrigues, and human connivance. Agnes, by the time the Franciscans arrived in Prague, had decided that a life of prayer and seclusion was the better road. At various periods she had been sent to Cistercian monasteries that functioned much like a "finishing school" for a future queen. The lessons learned in those houses struck a deep chord. With the friars came the possibility of founding a new convent of women following the forms of the Abbess Clare in Assisi.

From the start, major decisions that would shape the life of Agnes and her sisters were taken under the joint oversight of King Wenceslaus and Gregory IX. The wealth of her endowment was enormous. Thus, it was important to the crown and to the Holy See to control how poverty would be observed in Agnes's convent and how she would dispense her wealth. Pope Gregory, to be sure, wanted his Rule with its offer of stable possessions to be the form of profession. Agnes stood firm. Gregory argued with all his might to convince her of the folly of such a choice. He went so far as to describe the Rule of Francis as "milk for nursing babies"—not a proper monastic rule at all!

While Agnes insisted that she would follow the Clarian program, she exercised great originality in the architecture and status of her monastery. The convent of Prague was the opposite of the humble San Damiano. Agnes created a large complex that included a hospital, friary, major church, and sisters' convent. She entrusted the project to architects skilled in the design of Cistercian monasteries and churches. The chapel was to house the sepulchers of the royal family and, for that reason, it was modeled on the royal burial chapel in Paris. It did, in fact, serve as the burial place of King Wenceslaus in 1253.

Over a twenty-year period, Agnes deepened her dedication to the original Clarian program. Four letters from Clare tell us the story—though only in part. For the rest, we must cobble together the evidence from papal letters and decrees. What is clear is that Agnes, though her monastery had a unique political and ecclesial profile, was determined to bind herself and her community to the strictest interpretation of Clare's program. Clare addressed her in language that betokened both her royal status and her sacrificial witness—witness that reflected the life of her martyred patroness, Agnes of Rome. This Bohemian Agnes had famously declined multiple offers of a royal marriage and chose the road of evangelical poverty instead of dynastic luxury. The letters reveal the awe she inspired in Clare. As time passed, they included sisterly advice on practical matters such as fasting and ways that the abbess should conduct herself. They reveal a deep level of liturgical–poetical sensibility as Clare plays upon words drawn from the feast day liturgy of Saint Agnes. Clare gives free rein to her own deepest experiences of contemplative insight in these writings, intended as they are for a single person to whom she opened her soul with trusting simplicity.

Another trusted companion was to exercise an important role in the "resistance" of the two abbesses. Elias of Cortona was their bridge and loyal brother.

Gregory IX died in 1241, to be followed by Celestine, whose death took place within months. It was then that Innocent IV came to the papal throne. After Clare's death, Pope Innocent IV granted Agnes and her monastery the right to observe the Rule that he had approved for Clare. This approval crowned a long and dramatic battle waged by Agnes for the right to renounce her possessions and those of her monastery. Six years later, Alexander IV, the pope who canonized Clare, renewed this privilege. For twenty-two more years Agnes of Prague lived out this commitment as war and famine raged and her royal family suffered the consequences.

A 'Fast Forward' Note

Agnes's death in 1282 did not inaugurate a swift march to canonization. In fact, this plan was thwarted again and again by political and religious turmoil. It fell finally to St. John Paul II to canonize her on November 12, 1989. The ceremony took place in Rome. Communist authorities would not permit such an event to take place in Prague in spite of repeated requests. However, the same authorities in the Czech Republic and Slovakia did issue visas that allowed countless pilgrims to celebrate together in Rome.

Weeks later, the people of the Czech Republic broke the yoke of Soviet rule in what would come to be known as "the velvet revolution." If those citizens who had preserved the Catholic piety of earlier generations then claimed Agnes had liberated her homeland, they had good reason. Did the throngs gathered in Rome exercise their small oasis of freedom to consider a revolutionary reunion in the streets of Prague? Did the sight of countless faithful citizens crowding the Piazza San Pietro signal the possibility of a sea-change in Czech identity? In less than one month's time that reunion in Wenceslaus Square took place bringing Vaclav Havel to power and ending decades of Soviet oppression.

Over the centuries, Agnes's monastery was abandoned and sometimes reclaimed during wars, epidemics, political revolts. During the Soviet era it was saved from destruction and became an art museum. It functions in this way to this day.

Chapter Fifteen

ELIAS OF CORTONA

*I*n one of Clare's letters to Agnes she highlights the importance of Elias, General Minister, as a trusted advisor. This clue to the unique friendship of Clare and Elias sheds important light on the obscure twists and turns of the earliest Franciscan generation's experiences. Few of the early companions of Francis have sparked more controversy than Elias of Cortona. After losing his first designated successor, Peter Catanii, Francis placed the administration of the friars upon the shoulders of Brother Elias. His organizational abilities were evident. Early chronicles reveal a man who could support the vision of Francis but also make sure that the minutiae of daily operations in a growing brotherhood were skillfully handled. One historian noted that while Francis preached inspiring words to brothers gathered at chapters, it was probably Elias who made sure there was enough supper for those hundreds of hungry men when the sermon ended.

A major test of his leadership came at Francis's death. Making sure that the founder was both protected and cared for in his final months was no simple task. Guards were needed to prevent rival towns from holding the dying man as a hostage so that his death in their precincts would yield the right to keep his body. Elias arranged multiple trips in search of cures or rest in a favorite hermitage. The closest companions were on duty keeping watch in the final months.

At Francis's death, it fell to Elias to notify the brothers who now resided in many countries. That notification included the first official attestation of the miracle of the Stigmata. The movement from mourning to canonizing had been foreseen. Elias worked with the friar Thomas of Celano, a gifted theologian and writer, who was preparing official biographies to speed Francis's elevation to sainthood. Pope Gregory deputized Elias to start construction of a basilica to house the holy remains. The major construction was finished in one decade. The grand basilica, however, also became the cause of major discontents among the friars. Funds had to be raised and the pressures brought to bear upon friars to do this rankled many. The focus on getting financial support was bound to create serious tensions. How would Francis look upon this capital campaign conducted in his name? Many a brother was sure that Francis was already spinning in his temporary grave. When Elias orchestrated a secret transfer of Francis's remains to the new tomb, his stock fell, and resentments flared.

Nonetheless, Clare relied upon Elias as one of the companions whose closeness to Francis and to her monastery was a continued source of strength after Francis died. The misfortunes that befell him were surely so many thorns wounding her sisterly heart. Yet, the friendship did not fail. He continued to visit and to hold her trust. She had urged Agnes of Prague in her 1235 letter to follow the counsel of Elias. Her words are a dramatic and daring profession of trust:

> In all of this, follow the counsel of our venerable father, our Brother Elias, the Minister General, that you may

walk more securely in the way of the commands of the Lord. Prize it beyond the advice of others and cherish it as dearer to you than any gift. If anyone has said anything else to you or suggested any other thing to you that might hinder your perfection or that would seem contrary to your divine vocation, even though you must respect him, do not follow his commands. (*Second Letter to Agnes:* 15-17)

The "anyone" she refers to is none other than Pope Gregory IX!

As more ordained men became dominant in the government of the friars, the fact that a lay friar could command men in Holy Orders created a major contradiction of church law. Added to this was the fact that Elias was aligning with Emperor Frederick II in his struggles with the papacy. A witch's brew of discontent and opposition towards Elias finally boiled over. In 1239 Gregory IX took the fateful step of calling a chapter of the friars and removing Elias from office.

Elias died within the grace of God and the arms of the church. But his fate for centuries was to be vilified in the annals of Franciscan history. His hidden tomb in Cortona's church of St. Francis bore mute testimony to the level of alienation that continued after his death. Uncovering the story of Clare and their friendship offers powerful evidence that this brother's good was, indeed, "interred with his bones."

New ministers would now succeed to the leadership of the brothers. Each would contend with the political and pastoral demands being made upon the order with varying degrees of fidelity and fervor. Of none of these do we hear that the special support due to Clare and her community was cultivated. What we do know is that a number of those brothers who were part of Francis's inner circle maintained loyal ties and still others would work to support the constantly expanding realm of the Poor Sisters.

Chapter Sixteen

MIRACLES AND MARVELOUS PROTECTION

Many people find the emphasis on miracles in the lives of saints to be a vestige of another era. These stories belong, we feel, in a medieval society that was easily astonished and too quickly convinced of divine interventions. Our view is that if something cannot be explained empirically, it is thought to be a bit much—if not a total fantasy. Yet, as we enter deeply into Clare's life, we find the miraculous recounted and we cannot ignore it. Most of these instances were recorded with the sworn testimony of eyewitnesses. The investigation prior to her canonization was conducted with clear legal protocols. The document of this investigation has been called simply, "The Process." In it we read the firsthand accounts of sisters who lived with her and citizens in Assisi who knew her and her family. This record gives us the official sources for her story as distinct from those tales that depended upon folklore and oral transmission. What does "The Process" tell us?

Healings

Clare's miraculous interventions came in four distinct forms. The first dealt with healing a serious illness. There are fourteen such events. While some appeared to have occurred rather instantly, many more were the product of a long period of suffering on the part of the one afflicted. Clare did not wave a magic wand each time one of her sisters fell ill. When asked to offer her healing touch, she would make the Sign of the Cross over the sufferer and effect the cure. This sign seemed to be the culmination of prayer and fasting and humble intercession on Clare's part. Most of the miracles described were worked among her own sisters. For Sister Cristiana the gift was healing deafness in one ear. For Sister Benvenuta, it was healing a fistula that afflicted her for almost thirteen years. For Sister Andrea, Clare first ordered that she drink a tonic of boiled egg to ease the pain of a throat tumor. That home remedy was, however, the first phase of a complete healing that followed. Other sisters experienced similar release from fevers, abscesses, sore throats, and other crippling ailments.

Many people came to San Damiano for medical help. The little hospice offered many forms of nursing care that were within the range of normal remedies. But there were also healings deemed to be miracles. A woman possessed by five demons. A friar suffering mental torment. Another young boy in the grip of a dangerous fever. At least one sister reminded the church officials that many afflicted persons came to the monastery but not every healing was recorded. It is not easy to assign dates to these events. A good number appeared to have occurred in later years of her life—especially those related to her sisters. What is clear is that San Damiano was a place known to be a source of help for the sick dating to Roman times. Under Clare's leadership that ancient legacy was restored. Help was given to all who came; for some, that help was experienced as a miracle—a result far beyond human capacity to effect.

Attack and Siege

A second set of wonders was the prevention of armed attacks on the monastery and the Commune of Assisi. These two events display Clare's heroic courage and profound trust in God's providence. The first such attack took place in 1240. Emperor Frederick II was determined to restore the imperial hold on Assisi. (In the constant tug of war between pope and emperor, Assisi was on the papal side.) His military troops included mercenaries who were known as Saracens. A band of these soldiers managed to gain entrance into the enclosure of San Damiano. The sisters were overwhelmed by terror. They rushed to Clare and begged her to pray for help. She was no less fearful than they but focused on her need to protect them. She told them to bring the pyx that held the Eucharistic host to her. Holding the vessel, she implored Christ to come to their aid. As soon as her prayer was uttered, she heard a voice that assured her: "I will always defend you." At least one other sister later testified that she, too, heard the voice, though not all of those present did. It is not clear how Clare became visible to the intruders. The dramatic moment has been depicted in many paintings and she is often shown at a window or door holding the vessel aloft. The soldiers are shown beating a hasty retreat, their faces revealing their fright. We have no testimony from the intruders, so we are left to wonder just how this action by Clare inspired such a rout, such a happy reversal of fortune. (There is an echo here of the sudden departure of the knights attempting to kidnap her sister, Catherine.)

Just one year later another armed invasion was imminent. This time the citizens of Assisi understood that Vitale d'Aversa planned a siege of the commune. It was his intention to finally subdue the town for the emperor. Clare, upon hearing this very credible threat, convened the sisters. This time they would offer unceasing penitential prayer for the city. To signify the gravity of the situation, Clare removed her veil and covered her head in ashes—a time-honored gesture of a penitent's contrition. She then asked each sister to do the same, and she blessed each tonsured head with the ashes. The sisters' prayers were no doubt filled with the memories of the traumatic invasion they had recently endured. Their vigil of intercession was maintained night and day. Before long, the siege was lifted. The people credited the prayers of the sisters with this miracle. Clare, like so many cloistered women, thus became wedded to the welfare of her city. Hers was a citizenship of spiritual and moral solidarity which yielded real benefits to her neighbors.

Daily Needs and Difficulties

A third category of Clare's miracles can be seen in several events of daily life transformed by the power of her prayers. Early in the founding period of the small sisterhood, the supply of oil ran out. This was bad news for any household. Oil was critical to food preparation, for lighting, for medicinal needs. Clare requested one of the brothers who worked with the sisters to go out to find or beg for a new supply. When he arrived to pick up the large oil jar, it was full. Aggravated by what he assumed was a prank, he complained openly. Soon it was discovered that no one at the monastery had touched the vase once it was put in place. The appearance of the plentiful oil came from on high. On another occasion—in later years when there were fifty sisters there—the food supply was low. Clare instructed a worried sister to provide bread for the whole lot by slicing a small half loaf. While the sister cook replied that it would take a miracle such as Jesus worked in multiplying the loaves and fishes, she accepted her "mission impossible." The result? Her small loaf did not disappear until fifty portions were sliced and ready for the meal.

Perhaps the two events that form bookends of Clare's own physical endurance were the initial opening of the barred door when she escaped her home. Those who knew of that escape could not explain how she managed to open the door unaided. In later years, a large door of the monastery fell right on Clare. The cries of a nearby sister brought helpers running. It took three friars to lift the massive portal, but Clare was unharmed and described being thus covered as being under a warm blanket! Once again, her sisters could only wonder at the Providence that overshadowed her.

Wonders

These are the miracles that we find in a legal record. A fourth category can be found in a variety of imaginative stories that come from later chronicles. One of these is the collection of stories known as *The Little Flowers of St. Francis* or *The Fioretti*. This collection was published almost a century after the death of Francis. It is full of stories that reflect the wonder, joy, and simplicity of the first generations of sisters and brothers. While its historical *bona fides* are questionable, its appeal has given thousands a taste of that springtime of faith and fervor that Francis and Clare created.

Here we find story of her being invited by the Pope to offer a blessing for a meal while he was present as her guest. Naturally such deference by a pontiff was in itself miraculous, but that gesture was magnified when—at Clare's benediction—the form of a cross suddenly appeared on the bread set out for the meal. Another was the story of her joining Francis for a meal at the Portiuncula, which was described earlier. While they conversed about the gracious love of God manifest in their lives, others reported seeing them enveloped in a great fire. When neighbors came running to extinguish the flames visible at a distance, they found only the two holy ones on fire with God's love. If the story owes more to folklore than to fact, its allure remains. Its metaphor invites us to believe that what was lost when a fiery sword closed the gate of Eden may still be found again. Francis and Clare recover our lost home where daily converse with God fires our lives.

Visions and Voices

There are few accounts of Clare experiencing visions that take her out of the space-time continuum of other mortals. Here we come to a final form of miraculous happenings. We have seen that she had mystical experiences in which she appears caught up in another dimension. These were exceptional events and the reports leave little factual descriptions to allow us to understand what she was seeing and hearing in those trances. During the attack of the Saracens she clearly heard the voice of God—and at least one other sister heard the very same words. Another example was the vision of a sister who saw a beautiful child—a boy—with her while a sermon was being preached. Clare often spoke of the Mother of Jesus and cited their poverty in Bethlehem as motive for maintaining material poverty. The presence of a Divine Child at her side, something experienced more than once, points to her devotion to the Christ's infancy and childhood. Finally, we have a visionary experience that created a modern application. She wanted to join the brothers for the midnight Mass of Christmas at the Basilica of St. Francis. She was too ill to go there. When the sisters returned from their own prayers and began to describe the lovely liturgy, she informed them that she had been granted a visionary experience in which she saw— as if present in the basilica—the solemnities of Christmas. It is this remembrance from her life that led to her being named the patron saint of television!

Following Clare's death and even before her canonization, the faithful began to pray at her tomb. The miracles attested to by countless visitors to her tomb fill other records and give us to understand that Clare, no less than Francis, was seen as a powerful intercessor for the faithful.

Clare's Monstrance, a Post-Script

One postscript to this summary of her miracles is important. Many Catholics have seen statues or pictures of Clare holding a monstrance. The image comes from the story of the Saracen invasion. However, it is clear that such a sacred vessel was not yet in use. The witnesses describe a pyx—a small wooden receptacle for a host that was encased in ivory—as the vessel she held aloft to confront the attackers. However, many statues or paintings show her holding a large monstrance. (A monstrance is a large and beautifully decorated vessel. It normally consists of a round glass "window "to display the sacred Host which is mounted in the center of a cross.) Does the very existence of this image suggest a desire to preserve the memory of Clare—and medieval women like her—whose contemplation of the Eucharist conferred extraordinary status? Devotions like the feast of Corpus Christi, the Sacred Heart, veneration of the reserved Eucharist, the identification through fasting with the Heavenly Banquet—these practices emerged in this historic period. Such an image—while not historically accurate—has another function. It reminds us that women, who were forbidden to touch the Eucharist as did ordained men, nevertheless risked life and limb in their utter reverence for Christ's presence in the Bread of Life. They hold the mystery in their hands by mystical identification, not by legal jurisdiction. Such artistic images preserve memories at once dynamic and dangerous.

Chapter Seventeen

PENITENTIAL PRACTICES

*I*f modern sensibility balks at miracle stories, even more so will the descriptions of Clare's physical acts of penance trouble us. Her title, Abbess of Penitents, sounds a note of high praise, but the severity of her physical penances creates a chilling effect. Ours is an age focused on well-being, fitness, and self-care. The extremes of renunciation that we find in women like Clare and men like Francis are repellent to us. In fact, we tend to gloss over these portions of the story thinking that, perhaps, these were pious exaggerations meant to gratify readers of another time. So, we need to make a special effort to understand what we know of Clare's harsh bodily mortifications.

Her acts of self-denial did not begin after her escape from home. Even as a youngster she exhibited a pattern of giving up her own food or comforts to take care of the needy. Once ensconced in San Damiano she fasted in dramatic ways. It is reported that she ate nothing on several days of each week. On a Sunday, she would allow herself a small repast. This renunciation of food worries us given its parallels with the affliction of anorexia. Was Clare suffering from an illness or making a rational choice? Recent studies show that such extreme fasting was not uncommon among female mystics of the Middle Ages.

Research on the meaning of these female fasting practices gives us a window onto a culture far from our own but one that has its own internal coherence. Many holy women fasted to excess and attracted disciples who accepted their spiritual teaching. (Jacques de Vitry was one such disciple of the beguine Marie d'Oignies.) Profound self-denial was understood to be participation in the mystery of Christ's sufferings. Unable to enact heroic sacrifices of the crusaders or itinerant reformers, the women "transubstantiated" their own bodily capacities to express heights of spiritual desire. When in 1220 five friars were martyred in Morocco for their Christian preaching, Clare responded by declaring that she would take up their aborted mission. So adamant was she about wanting to imitate the martyrs' sacrifice that the sisters were clearly frightened that she might actually fulfill that ardent desire. Denied the possibility of such active preaching of the Gospel, the fasting she and others endured was a substitute expression of "losing one's life" for Jesus's sake.

However, it appears that Clare's fasting, even if motivated by spiritual ideals, was not supported by those closest to her. Francis, along with the bishop, visited her to demand that she alter her practice. The fact that he invoked the authority of the church in this instruction indicates how very worried he was and how determined he was to make sure that she would comply. In other words, his own efforts prior to this meeting had not been successful. Clare's illnesses that seem to be omnipresent from early on appear to have their roots in this excessive fasting.

She used a physical garment called a hair shirt worn against her skin. These were vest-like garments fashioned of the skin of a pig or horse with the bristles intact so that they lacerated the flesh they rubbed against. This was a practice of many ascetics. That a woman born among nobles would be capable of enduring such continual torment astounded not only her sisters, but the brothers as well. One account describes a sister asking Clare's permission to wear a similar penitential garment. She gave up quickly and declared that she could not believe that Clare could endure such pain and maintain her good disposition.

Clare and the others endured other privations. Food was not always plentiful and stock supplies such as bread and oil were, at times, depleted. The bedding and garments they had were hardly equal to the cold and damp that winter on the slopes of Mount Subasio brought with it. The garments she wore were made of cloth that was described as "vile"—a word chosen to denote the clothing of the poorest people. It was, in other words, nothing that a woman of good breeding would wear with comfort or pleasure. The images of her dress in Assisi's ancient frescoes result from an "air brushing" of her actual garments. In those portraits she is a well-dressed nun regarding us with a grave and lovely countenance.

Living with a large number of women who are not kin is its own call to penance. While the major impression of the San Damiano community is one of concord, joyful obedience, and humility, the opposite vices were not unknown. Why else would Clare have found it necessary to outline specific punishments for those who transgressed? She writes that the sisters must beware of "pride, vainglory, envy, avarice, care and anxiety about this world, detraction and murmuring, dissension and division" (Rule 10:6 [19]). This is a sobering litany of faults capable of destroying a community from inside. What experiences showed her the need for such an admonition? What reports from other monasteries might have confirmed the need for that warning? We should not imagine the forty years in San Damiano to have been devoid of such suffering. These were real flesh and blood women. Their virtues are on display in the formal biographies, but their vices are backlit in the Rule's chapter of "admonition and correction."

One thing that her earliest companions wanted to pass on when asked to testify about her life was the assertion that her disposition was always one of peaceful composure. Her privations did not result in making her short-tempered, gloomy, or cold. She exhibited an inner joy in all circumstances. This demeanor added to the awe of her companions and became part of their endless admiration. This "peace surpassing understanding" drew them daily into her orbit of sisterly solidarity.

Chapter Eighteen

TEACHING AND WRITING

Clare's work included daily instruction of the sisters. When they spoke later about this, their recollection was joyful. What did her instructions contain? Since many of these teachable moments probably took place during chapter meetings, let's look at the chapter's function. (The term *chapter* is shorthand for a formal meeting of a community that begins by reading a chapter of the Rule. It simply means a formal meeting of the gathered community.) The chapter could serve more than one purpose. It might be a solemn event for the election of a new abbess or dealing with a significant decision. It might be an ordinary gathering meant to review the work to be done and make assignments. It might be a "chapter of faults" in which the members of the community publicly confessed the ways in which they failed to observe the rule itself or the directives meant to insure order in a big community. Clare would have been able to convene sisters in such chapters to give instructions but also to provide lessons on how they might improve their own practice of virtue.

The Teacher

Her Rule speaks of young girls who live in the monastery but are not old enough to make a vow. They may have been girls who wanted to join the sisters. They would be permitted to live in the monastery and be educated there. They may also have been "offered" to the community by parents unable to provide for their children. (Sister Lucia was one such sister who came to the monastery as a child.) They might have been abandoned or orphaned and given to the sisters for care. Such practice was widespread in the Middle Ages. Gregory IX legislated that the age of profession was twelve for a girl and fourteen for a boy. The young girl, offered in this way before reaching the legal age, would be free to leave if she did not wish to become a member of the monastery. However, she would have been the beneficiary of the practical and spiritual training received there.

For these younger girls, particular teaching responsibilities would be delegated to other sisters. For the community of professed sisters continual instruction provided ample guidance for personal holiness and common observances. An abbess with particular intellectual and spiritual gifts would amplify this curriculum.

The Writings

The number of Clare's writings that were preserved are a precious inheritance. Those that get the most attention are her four letters to Agnes of Prague written in 1234, 1235, 1238, and 1253. Were there others that were lost? What happened to letters from Agnes to Clare? The Rule was completed by 1252. It is a major repository of the obligations of the sisters' chosen life and the spirit in which those obligations were to be fulfilled. (We will learn more about this text in a later chapter.) A Testament—a kind of spiritual autobiography—is thought to have been written in her final years. Some experts question its authenticity and suggest that it was written after her death but circulated as if written by her. The motive for such an ambitious ruse might have been to call the sisters to more pristine observance at a time of reform. The Blessing is a beautiful text believed to reflect her wishes for her sisters as her end drew near.

There are two writings associated with Clare that cannot be proven to be from her hand. One is a Prayer to the Five Wounds of the Lord. Since it was stated that she did prize such a devotion, it is not surprising that an old manuscript of it has been preserved. A letter sent to a religious woman named Ermentrude who lived in the city of Bruges is the last. Again, Clare's authorship is no longer accepted. However, it echoes the main themes of her spiritual life and its simple language breathes a spirit of the vernacular teaching that was so important in the Franciscan milieu.

Finally, a text that gets almost no attention is included in official collections. It is called the Mandate and dated at 1238. It is a legal document that authorizes a business agent of the monastery to sell land to the Canons (clergy) of San Rufino—the cathedral of Assisi. There is a precise description of the land in question and equally precise description of the rights and duties of the agent in completing the transaction. An intriguing detail is the clarity of referring to the community members as either "ladies" or "sisters." It is an important detail. These women did not use the title that would be the equivalent of the modern religious title of "sister" or "mother." They used the lay terms that designated social status of nobility (ladies) or lack of noble inheritance (sisters). The signature of the abbess was all that was required for the validity of the sale. Yet it was signed by every sister. This detail is touching and revealing; Clare habitually spoke of working "together with my sisters." Here, she gave each sister—whether of noble rank or not—the right to be a signatory. All had the same status as sisters in community. Actually, this is an enormous clue about the attraction that her form of life exercised for women whose voices had no civil weight, no place in the councils of the rising commune. There, in the small feminine fortress of San Damiano, voice and vote were assured to everyone.

Each of these texts can be studied over and over. Many a contemporary writer has done just that and offered a great deal of theological exploration of Clare's writings. Details of the Rule and admonitions in the Letters show something of the particular situations she and the sisters faced. Finally, these texts confirm that Clare had a level of education and literacy that was exceptional for a woman of the thirteenth century. It has been noted by more than one scholar that her capacity for writing in Latin was more refined than that of Francis, whose education was limited to what was needed for mercantile operations. Her capabilities were exceptional. Did she also have assistance from others—sisters or friars—whose education might have exceeded her own? We do not know. What is cause for rejoicing is that her voice can find us after all of these centuries through these texts.

Chapter Nineteen

JESUS CRUCIFIED, THE MIRROR

Neither Francis nor Clare offered their companions a systematic manual of prayer. Clearly, they believed that the established form of the Divine Office was of paramount importance. By faithful recitation each day, the brother or sister was immersed in the Psalter, readings from Old and New Testaments, hymns and readings that related the lives of the saints and the teaching of the great Church fathers. While they favored some unique rituals and practices, there was little made obligatory beyond the normal liturgical cycle of Office and Mass and the primacy of time for personal meditation. The over-arching theme that ties all of the prayers and devotions together centers on the Passion of Christ.

The Book of the Cross

This theme runs through her entire life—the motif of a plaintive melody. Even before she put this experience into words, Clare lived into the mystery of Christ's sufferings in the timing of her departure from Assisi. Her Palm Sunday exodus placed her act of renunciation in the midst of the liturgical drama of Holy Week. She joined "the new army of the poor," and left the city where her armed relatives would demand her return to the Babylon of their wealthy existence. As the days of Holy

Week with its Passiontide readings passed, she faced familial outrage and rejection. She found herself a stranger in a large religious house whose ways were unfamiliar. Surely the confrontation with Monaldo and his troops created a tension with her Benedictine hostesses. The nuns must have been unhappy to have their high holy days disturbed like that. One can imagine their abbess counselling patience and generous forbearance as their noble guest worked out her first steps as a penitent sister. Clare, meanwhile, knew the meaning of the invitation from Hebrews: "Let us then go to him outside the camp, bearing the reproach that he bore. For here we have no lasting city but we seek the one that is to come" (Hebrews 13:13).

When she entered San Damiano, she came into possession of the beautiful Byzantine cross before which Francis had prayed. Now it was her "book" of prayer, her silent reminder each day: "Take up your cross and follow me." In that Face, she saw mirrored the love that would insist that one who lays down a life is the greatest of Friends and the model of all Christian friendship. The story of redemption portrayed on the Cross helped her to anchor her soul in that mystery. One speaks of "reading" an icon. What did Clare read in that Cross? She found the images of those who accompanied Jesus to Calvary, the angels mourning the outrage they witness, the centurion piercing that beloved Heart with his lance. There, too, she would see the image of Christ ascending back to the heavenly firmament—his Father's hand outstretched to welcome him after his quest to save humanity was completed. Most of all, she would spend hours contemplating that Face. The expression is one of serene and salvific love. The body is not writhing in agony, but is glorified, having conquered death's destructive force. In the annual Easter liturgies, she would hear the chanted refrain: "I have risen and am with you." Through this Cross that beautiful melody was manifested every day of her life.

Francis's Office of the Passion

As we see in her writings, the theme of connection with Christ's passion was constant. She wrote to Agnes:

> If you suffer with Him, you will reign with Him, weeping with Him you will rejoice with Him; dying on the cross of tribulation with Him, you will possess heavenly mansions with Him among the splendor of the saints and in the Book of Life your name will be called glorious among the peoples. (Second Letter, 21-22)

There was a Holy Week in which she entered into a mystical trance from which she recovered only after two days. The sisters clearly understood that her stupor was actually a mystical experience of living the days with Christ—an experience from which she emerged as one returning from another world.

While there are very few special devotions attributed to her, one is a prayer to the Five Wounds of Jesus. She regularly prayed the Office of the Passion that Francis composed. This liturgical prayer was an elaborate composition that led the praying sister or brother to meditation on Christ's journey to Calvary. Francis designed this Office and modeled it on the normal hours of the Divine Office, which was required of all of his followers. The Office of the Passion was rooted in the practice of seeing each of the required hours of prayer as parallel to the chronology of the hours of Jesus's suffering. Thus, the one praying entered into the mind of Jesus, seeking to identify with him as he prayed the psalms during his ultimate humiliation. The one praying could follow him in spirit from Gethsemane to the Holy Sepulcher. Each hour consisted of a psalm with antiphons and short prayers as a framework. Each psalm came from the biblical psalter, but Francis rearranged the verses to reflect how he imagined Jesus would pray at each of those hours. Thus, the psalms are filled with lament, with expressions of fear, of desire to be spared, to be protected from one's enemies. At the same time, they proclaim trust in the loving will of the Father, and confidence in ultimate salvation.

Clare's writings often include the metaphor of a mirror. In Francis's body she beheld a stark mirror of the Passion. She then taught the sisters how clearly they must pattern their lives on that of Jesus. He had to become their Mirror. Her fourth letter to Agnes of Prague includes this appeal:

> Therefore, that Mirror, suspended on the wood of the Cross, warned those passing by that here are things to be considered saying: "All you who pass by the way, look and see if there is any suffering like my suffering!" Let us respond to Him, it says, "crying out and lamenting, in one voice, in one spirit: 'Remembering this over and over leaves my soul sinking within me!' (Fourth Letter, 24-26)

III

Chapter Twenty

THE FINAL DECADE

*I*f Clare's work during her midlife focused on guiding her small but growing network of monasteries, her final decade would be centered on finalizing her Rule. Multiple events and the astute observations of the abbess were leading her to recognize that it was now her turn to prepare a text that could stand the test of time—and that of the church authorities.

Within four years of Francis's death, the friars had to send a delegation of brothers to Rome to seek clarification of questions about their Rule from Pope Gregory IX. Once that event took place an inevitable reliance on papal authority to settle any disputed matter became the friars' chosen path. The papacy, clearly in need of the friars' wonderful work of evangelization, was only too happy to provide such help even when it meant controversial departures from the founder's practice. Once papal interpretation became the default solution for major disagreements, the pristine insights of Francis became overlaid with volumes of new restrictions (or relaxations) issued from the Lateran.

Clare witnessed this evolution and understood it. She faced the evidence that the original ideals were under assault—even if from persons who believed their assault was actually a work of prudent adaptation.

Pope Innocent IV, elected in 1243, was issuing new permissions for the Friars Minor. These were meant to allow more sensible access to money and property. The method involved appointment of lay business agents who would spare the friars the difficulty of acting contrary to the Rule but would manage monetary transactions for them. It was a delicate dance, even for a pope. The friars certainly did not seek wholesale abandonment of their strong commitment to poverty. However, the obligations created by their commitment to the church's needs required new solutions. If they needed to study to be approved as preachers, where would they live and what library possessions might they need? If they worked among people who would not permit them to beg due to local economic conditions—as was the case in England— how would they manage to meet basic needs? The sunlit freedom of the earliest days of the brotherhood was long gone. Now the friars who felt obliged to keep that memory alive found themselves on the margins as new generations demanded more accommodations to enhance their successful apostolic work.

Soon Clare had direct experience of this papal program for tidying up problematic aspects of Franciscan legislation. Innocent IV not only gave the friars new freedoms in his directives, he now authored a new rule for the Poor Sisters. We can only imagine the astonishment of Clare and her sisters upon receiving this latest pontifical attempt to undermine —with best intentions—her leadership.

It was becoming clearer what would befall her sisters after her death. If the constant pressure that the church authorities exerted to get her to accept a different rule was this constant during her life, what hope was there that a future generation of Poor Sisters could resist? If the "Order of St. Damian" continued to be the preferential option of papal power, what confusion of ends and means would face women who wished to be part of this sisterhood in years to come? Perhaps her own sisters urged action upon her. They, too, would have been anxious and alert to the reality that Clare was the first and strongest defense against these threats. The regard in which ecclesiastical princes held her would vanish with her into the grave. Then what? Then would come the time when a clear set of instructions for the life of the poor sisters would be an essential tool for protecting their privileges.

The first companions of Francis remained close to Clare. Among those were three—Leo, Angelo and Rufino—who collected their personal memories of Francis in writing at the formal request of their Minister. This collection was turned over to the Order's head, Crescentius, in 1246. Thus, a "return to the beginnings" was now preserved in writing. The "three companions," as they came to be known, adopted a theme we might translate like this: "We were with Francis. *We* know the whole unabridged story. We'll show these newcomers what *real* Franciscan life looks like." These aging friends of the Poverello were desperate to communicate his actual words and examples. In this way they hoped to stem the growing trend of mitigation. Leo, in particular, was a custodian of these important documents. Their written work was done. Hers was just beginning.

The dramatic changes taking place among the brothers, the papal attempts at new regulations, the feverish attempts to collect authentic reports of Francis's words and deeds—this was a potent mix motivating Clare to act. The time had come for her to face up to the challenge of a final written Rule and Life for her sisters.

Chapter Twenty-One

THE BOND OF PERFECTION

The simple and straightforward *Form of Life* given by Francis must now become the cornerstone of a different kind of document, a rule such as those approved in ancient times and more recently the Rule of Francis. Such a document had to meet certain criteria for approval and be submitted to church authority for confirmation. It was not a private affair. What were the elements she would incorporate? Who were the advisors she would summon in order to achieve this?

She had the sources upon which her community had depended for thirty years. The original *Form of Life* and the *Last Will* from Francis held first place. The *Audite* of Francis—an appeal that had chivalrous overtones of concern and protective affection—was a treasured reminder to maintain their *esprit d'corps*. The Rule of Francis approved for the friars' observance in 1223 along with the earlier Rule document of 1221 provided important content for her consideration. As she had always worked in harmony with the brothers, knowledge of how they experienced the evolution of their own Rule were likely topics of conversation over the years. Perhaps Brother Leo served as a primary source and confidante as she undertook this work.

The Rule of Cardinal Hugolino-Gregory IX was a major influence for the sisters. Still, it was not the soul of their enterprise.

Where the rule of Hugolino-Gregory IX would impose a discipline that could lead to dry formalism, she would craft an expression to define observance with a different tone of voice.

The endless stream of formal documents from the papacy to women's monasteries hemmed them in but did not quench the inner fires of their commitment. Then there was the matter of the Rule of Innocent IV. Here was one more instance in which the Poor Sisters had to send their carefully worded response of filial gratitude to the pope with the firm declaration that they could in no way submit to the provisions that he dictated. Yes, he had assured the formal bond with the friars and that was a major legal breakthrough. However, he also ruled that they would accept property and securities they had long ago foresworn. Once more, Clare had to stand upon the ramparts.

If ever there is a dramatic production that portrays these continual exchanges between San Damiano and the pope's Lateran Palace it will require gifted actors. They will have to portray the continued amazement and aggravation of those powerful men who despaired of finding a way to get agreement from these women. How was it possible that their superior education and pontifical privileges did so little to persuade these nuns to comply? How was it possible to punish a woman whose identification with the now-sainted Francis was so unique? Many a *brento* of wine must have been drained in the papal dining hall when these responses from Assisi arrived. One can sympathize with a pontiff who simply needed to find efficient solutions for the interminable complications among the Franciscans but who found himself checkmated like this. In spite of his frustration, Innocent recognized that Clare was the most admired and beloved witness to the life of *Il Santo*. This called for care and respect.

The example of other women's monasteries influenced her work. The traditions of Benedictine convents provided pragmatic examples. Frequent chapters for the abbess to consult every sister openly became the norm. The abbess was to provide sufficient food and clothing to prevent breakdowns in health—guidance that echoed Benedict's wise counsel to avoid extremes. The conduct of visitors and the limits of access to inner sections of the monastery were prescribed. The sanctions against a member guilty of major infractions needed to be spelled out.

New expressions of female holiness found in small communities of *beguines* or *bizzoche* demonstrated the capacity of women in search of new wineskins. These houses of penitents created attractive options for women, especially those coming from the *minores*. They exhibited the enterprising spirit of their milieu. There were holy women whose reputation travelled far beyond their convent walls. They authored new devotional practices to be taught and widely propagated. Devotion to the sacrament of the Eucharist, to the Sacred Heart and to the sufferings of the Passion arose in this ferment. (So strong was this current of spirituality that it literally transformed the art that depicted the Crucified. When these women commissioned new crosses for their chapels, the image moved from the still and serene Byzantine body of the glorified Christ to the tortured and twisted limbs of the Man of Sorrows.) While such currents did not have direct impact upon this Rule, this spirit of open searching for Gospel perfection was in the air and the exchanges among these women gave spirit and life to Clare's holy ambitions.

The shared experience of her sisters was a vessel of the Holy Spirit's work. Clare saw that the best religious rule comes not from hierarchical directives but from human experience of the Holy Spirit's power working beyond imagining. Such wisdom was the shared treasure of the sisters who, over the course of years, had learned what constituted a form of life that was stable and realistic. Such a rule guaranteed a life of holiness that was joy-filled and self-sacrifice that was generative. Her rule must be invested with the sisterly convictions that the women of San Damiano shared. Indeed, San Damiano functioned as a centrifuge that was drawing all of these sources into a new amalgam of feminine Franciscan practice.

She knew that she would incorporate those dictates that would insure papal approval. These would be details of monastic cloister, fasting, clothing, and relationships to the clergy and friars such as were found in the Hugolinian constitution. Too many skirmishes with the Curia had shown that if she failed to incorporate those elements, the new text would be rejected. Twenty-five years had passed since Francis submitted his first Rule to the Pope. It was filled with the poetry and passion of those first years. It became clear that the papal curia was not seeking poetry, but policy clearly delineated and capable of legal adjudication. She would not forget the sting of that refusal, and she would apply the lesson learned. She also experienced the unhappy results of failing to allow for human frailty in her early governing years. Francis certainly had. As the fruit of hard lessons learned, restrictions and sanctions would be spelled out.

The great challenge she faced was how to manifest her compliance with the church authority while preserving the core commitments of her sisterhood. These must be expressed in the specific spirit in which they were lived and transmitted to new members and new monasteries. For this, she had to make the most careful selection and diplomatic amendments. Even a casual reading of Hugolino's Rule demonstrates how very difficult this discernment had to be.

The oversight of the Cardinal Protector, Rainaldo, was a source of wise counsel in these matters. Clare needed to give assurance that the Poor Sisters were willing to comply with those non-negotiables. He would be an invaluable guide, helping her to meet the requirements for approval while respecting her unique concerns. The careful combination of original instructions from Francis with the canonical demands had to be skillfully managed. Clare need not labor alone but could rely on his sage advice.

Her Rule and Life, once complete, does exhibit the presence of more than once voice. This was not a weakness to her way of thinking but the result of her careful design of many threads. What she longed to do was insure that the Voice that dominated would be the one that called daily from the pages of Scripture: "Put on then, as God's chosen ones, holy and beloved, heartfelt compassion, kindness, humility, gentleness, and patience, bearing with one another and forgiving one another.... And over all these put on love which is the bond of perfection" (Colossians 3:12-14).

Chapter Twenty-Two

WEAVING WITH WORDS

With this wealth of material and experience Clare leaned in to the task of formulating her ultimate insurance policy. Since the document to be prepared had to meet the requirements for ecclesiastical approval, she may well have invited the help of a scribe accustomed to such work. Brother Leo had written so many of the documents that preserved Francis's writings and deeds. Might he have been not only an advisor but her amanuensis as well? While another hand may have created the physical document, its contents would mirror her way of thinking about the life at San Damiano.

As she had labored over the years in doing the fine handwork that helped support the monastery, she now set herself the task of a written text. As with the many hours spent creating corporals and altar linens using needle and thread, she made a plan for her design. Her threads were the various strands of regulation and admonition, imitation of other exemplars, and the hard-won wisdom of her sisters. Each of these threads had its own color, its own heft and weight, its own role to play in creating her design. She would center the most important words of all, Francis's dictates, in the most vivid colors. These would be encased within a carefully tailored web of words of darker threads that manifested obedience to pontiff and church. For that reverence was also at the heart of the Franciscan way and the threads of somber color conveyed the solemn obligation. Small hints of color and original stitchery would reflect the unique San Damiano spirit, the evidence of women's ways of walking in Jesus's footprints.

As she had always consulted the sisters on matters that touched the lives of all, she now could invite them to discern with her the precise wording of difficult passages. We can imagine the spirited conversations and debates of those chapters. How might the text express their obligations? How best might she mirror the intent of the Hugolinian Rule without giving room to the negative view of human sinfulness that dominated so many of its passages. How could she capture the kernel of canonical thought while doing away with the hard shell in which it was encased? Let us eavesdrop on the discussion as Clare presents the difficult passages to be included.

> HUGOLINO: [Speaking of women who come to join…] the hard and austere realities…must be explained to all who wish to enter this religion and are received…lest ignorance be their excuse later on.

> SISTERS: If, by divine inspiration, anyone should come to us desiring to accept this life, the abbess is bound to seek the consent of all the sisters; let the tenor of our life be thoroughly explained to her.

> HUGOLINO: After they have entered the enclosure of this religion and have assumed the religious habit, they should never be granted permission or faculty to leave, unless perhaps some are transferred to another place to plant or build up this religion.

SISTERS: Thereafter she may not go outside the monastery except for a useful, reasonable, evident and justifiable purpose.

HUGOLINO: Let this [silence] be observed firmly by all, the sick as well as the healthy, so that they speak neither among themselves nor with others unless there are at least three persons present.

SISTERS: At all times, however, they may be permitted to speak with discernment in the infirmary for the recreation and service of the sick.

Thus, she and her sisters embroidered an enclosure of words chosen to protect their vision as surely as their stout outer walls. Little by little the work moved forward. As with Francis, the written record was firmly rooted in a lived experience. For that reason, Clare would not work in splendid isolation. She would offer multiple opportunities for the sisters and her closest advisors to help her shape the final results.

She completed the Rule by 1252. Cardinal Rainaldo, the Cardinal Protector, gave his signature in approval. His approval had the force of the papal authority which he represented and would have been sufficient to guarantee its permanent validity. Yet, something more was a secret desire of her heart. That desire was to be fulfilled in her last hours on earth.

Lacking a treasury of images of Clare's life to match the abundant frescoes in the Basilica of St. Francis, we must always be ready to create new visions and voices to fill that void. Our Franciscan poet laureate, Murray Bodo, OFM, has done just that to allow us to "see" Clare's ultimate project unfold before the eyes of our imagination.

St. Clare Writes a Rule of Life

Compared to intricate Benedict,
wordy Bernard of Clairvaux,
Francis's words are simple,
   threadbare
like the Gospel. She strokes
his original weave, runs practiced fingers
over his pattern, his twelve bare chapters.
She turns again to her diurnal
needlework, braids her sisters'
colored threads—yellows,
red and greens—around his brown.
She tightens the folds, hems,
double-stitches what can fray.
Like Host and chalice that weights
her altar cloth, she needle-points
the cloistered center of her Rule:
"The holy poverty we've promised
God and blessed Francis, neither
receiving nor possessing property,
except land enough for monastic
integrity, seclusion, and a garden
for the needs of the sisters."

—Murray Bodo, O.F.M.

Chapter Twenty-Three

CLARE'S DEATH

A year passed and Clare's health deteriorated even more. August 1253, with its scorching temperatures, found her closer and closer to the end. As always, the late summer heat drove the papal entourage from Rome's contagion to the refreshing heights of Perugia. It would not be long until these dignitaries heard the news echoing from hill to hill in the Valley of Spoleto: Madonna Chiara was dying.

Innocent IV understood the meaning of the moment. No doubt, his nephew Cardinal Rainaldo accompanied him on the journey to the little cloister. This pope, whose attempt at a rule for the women had been politely rejected by San Damiano's sisters, arrived to see its famous abbess. She received him with utter respect and humble gratitude. How wonderful was this? The successor of St. Peter was under her roof, offering his blessing and begging her prayers in return. He asked the crucial question: What was her deathbed wish? She was ready with her answer. Would he, in the fullness of his apostolic authority, place his signature and seal on her Rule? No question would ever be raised about its force and power if he were to comply with this one wish. Her plea was uttered with all of the force of a soul bent on completing its earthly mission. What was a pope to do?

What follows is a touching twenty-four-hour drama. The actual parchment upon which the text was inscribed and signed by Cardinal Rainaldo was at hand. Normal protocol would have required that an entirely new manuscript be prepared in the pope's secretariat. However, it was clear that there was not enough time if Innocent was to grant her wish before her final hour. His choice was to expedite the legal process. Using the manuscript already signed by Rainaldo, he added his own signature and date. To this was added his impressive seal. As he ordered it to be sent back, he reflected perhaps, that it would serve one monastery and one monastery only. No great harm done, therefore, in acceding to the dying wish of a respected abbess. Besides, it was a work of mercy that might win heavenly favor for him in an hour of need. Assisi's newest saint would surely intercede for him after death.

A friar messenger was dispatched to bring it back to Assisi with all possible speed. When the document was placed in her hands, Clare took hold of the beautiful papal seal, affixed with golden cords and hanging from the scroll. Later, an eyewitness would write on that parchment: "Blessed Clare touched and kissed this many times out of devotion." This elation expressed her utter relief and joy. She had succeeded in creating a perpetual witness to the first inspirations of the Poor Sisters and their covenant with Francis and his Lesser Brothers. Like her Divine Master, she could now say: "It is finished."

Visions of the Vigil

The extraordinary papal about face that took place in those August days was not the only miraculous event witnessed by the women keeping vigil with Clare in her final days. Those who were present would later recall other dramatic signs that they sealed in memory.

A nun in the Monastery of San Paolo shared an exceptional vision. In it she and her sisters were at the side of Clare who lay in a beautiful bed. They grieved with the distraught sisters keeping vigil. Then a woman of great beauty appeared at the head of the bed and assured the sisters that Clare's victory was assured and that she would not die without seeing "the Lord and His disciples." The fact that nuns of San Paolo had such vivid experiences of Clare's final days hints at a relationship that had blossomed over the years since her Eastertide sojourn in 1212.

Sister Benvenuta of Lady Diambra and Sister Anastasia heard Clare speaking softly at one point but to no one in particular. Worried that Clare was trying to express a need or discomfort, they asked to whom she was speaking. The answer was, "I am speaking to my soul." Later, the words they heard were recorded. Clare was, in fact, expressing the kind of hope that replaces fear with her trust in God to escort her over death's threshold as a mother guides a frightened child. Sister Filippa reported that Clare made a final confession and she marveled at what was told by the dying saint.

Three days before Clare's passing, Sister Benvenuta began to imagine the manner in which Clare would be received in heaven at the point of death. The imagining morphed into a visionary experience in which she saw a group of women—dressed in virginal white and wearing crowns—surround the bed. In the middle was one woman whose crown was larger and more ornate. The description implies that it was Mary, Queen of Heaven. The women brought a delicate, transparent coverlet to spread over Clare, a gesture reminiscent of women preparing a bridal bed.

In the dormitory of San Damiano is a bronze bas-relief on the wall where Clare died. It shows friars who are clearly bereft kneeling at her side. Her biographer tells us that Angelo was mourning and supporting the grieving sisters while Leo "kissed the bed of the dying woman." The placement of the sculpture is a reminder of the strength of that promise of care and solicitude that Francis made to Clare. His oldest friends carried that promise with them as they shared the *transitus* of their sister. Did they, in the long hours, recall the time when Francis himself set about repairing the crumbling structure of the place? It was his first project as a newly recognized penitent and he was offering his physical labor to the local priest. One day, hoping to recruit needed helpers, he climbed a wall and called out to passers-by. He declared that this rundown hospice would someday house holy women who would give glory to God. What was he thinking that day? Who could have imagined what had transpired in the hundreds of days since?

So it was that Clare, born of the house of Offreducio, breathed her last in the house of San Damiano on August 11, 1253. At her side were the women, seen and unseen, with whom she had established the Poor Sisters' way of life and the men whose loyal friendship was precious evidence of the mutuality that bound them. Clare would now belong not only to these brave founding men and women but to all future generations of Francis's followers who will promise to "hold onto the words, the life, the teaching and the Holy Gospel" of the Lord Jesus Christ (*Rule of 1221*, XXII, 41).

Chapter Twenty-Four

FROM SISTER TO SAINT

Once news of Clare's death was reported in the city, the people gathered at the monastery expressing grief comingled with wonder. Now their city boasted a second saint whose life would be that "light to the world" foretold to Lady Ortulana.

The funeral conducted in the city was a marvel. Since the whole papal entourage was nearby, its members accompanied Innocent IV to celebrate the funeral Mass. The pope startled his retinue by a proposal that the Mass of Holy Virgins be celebrated instead of a Requiem Mass. That choice would, in effect, be a canonization, an affirmation that Clare was officially recognized as a saint. The members of his court argued prudent restraint. Was it wise to ignore the protocols so recently ratified to insure the validity of canonization? Won over by these arguments, Innocent offered the traditional Mass for the dead with its supplications and lamentations. However, his readiness to raise Clare to official status as a saint was on full display. The insistence of his advisors was very good luck for future generations. It was that argument that led to the investigation whose record is such an important source for our knowledge of her.

She was buried in San Giorgio in the same crypt that had housed the remains of Francis until his tomb in the Basilica was ready. Unwilling to be separated from her even by death, four sisters relocated to the small cloister of San Giacomo di Muro Rupto so as to be able to keep prayerful vigils at her tomb. Thus began the transition that would take Clare from the center of a living sisterhood to the center of a cult bringing multitudes to pray in her sanctuary. In only two months' time, Innocent directed the Bishop of Spoleto to open the process for her canonization. In November Bishop Bartholomew arrived in Assisi to do his work. Over four days he and his staff interviewed fifteen of the sisters and five citizens of Assisi. The friars who participated—but who were not deposed—were Leo, Angelo, and Mark, the chaplain of San Damiano.

Innocent IV died the following month and was succeeded by none other than Cardinal Rainaldo who took the name Alexander IV. To him would fall the happy task of "raising Clare to the altar" which he did in 1255. The ceremony took place at another papal residence in Anagni. The Papal Decree of Canonization was a *tour de force* of verbal diplomacy. Poetic riffs on her name abound with synonyms for light. There are exclamations of astonishment at her miracles and a liberal use of wonderful metaphors: "a spring of water in the Valley of Spoleto," "a candelabra of sanctity," a "garden of humility." At the same time, the proclamation praises her fidelity to the hierarchical version of women's religious life and downplays the originality of her Franciscan loyalties. Thus, even in declaring her a saint, Alexander signaled the kind of obedience to be expected of future followers.

Five years later a new basilica in her honor was ready and her remains were interred there. The old San Giorgio church, once the place of Francis's early education and the temporary crypt for both saints, was incorporated into the new structure. The sisters, now led by the Abbess Benedetta, departed the San Damiano monastery and took up residence in the large cloister attached to the basilica. It would be known as the Proto-Monastery—the first of the monasteries of Poor Clares in the world. With them they brought the revered Cross whose Voice both saints obeyed.

In Our Time

As with St. Francis, the crypt of her burial was lodged deep in the lower recesses of the church far from the nave where pilgrims would venerate the high altar that surmounted the hidden tomb. In the late nineteenth century, a project to exhume her remains and excavate the crypt was approved. This modern innovation was taking place in each basilica. It was a way to afford pilgrims more direct proximity to the holy remains. For centuries medieval fears of kidnappings of a saintly sarcophagus had kept the actual tomb secret and remote. Now the pilgrim would be able to approach the resting place at arm's length.

Today, the visitor to Clare's basilica will see a sculpture that represents her body behind which is a vessel with her actual remains. Carefully renovated for her 1993 centenary, the image represents the body, which would have been placed there in 1261 and which was glimpsed fleetingly by those present at the exhumation. Nearby is a museum display that holds memorabilia of importance including her habit, the alb long thought to have been made by her, the parchment of the Rule, a breviary of St. Francis entrusted to Sister Benedetta by Brother Leo, and many other items that excite curiosity as much as they inspire reverence. If truth be told, many a pilgrim brushes past the documents and clothing in order to catch a glimpse of a glass vase containing her golden curls. It is a badge of our common humanity that the evidence of papal connections and holy devotions interests us less than the sight of her feminine adornment, her lovely hair covered for decades by a nun's veil.

Many metaphors have been employed to paint the picture of the relationship between Francis and Clare of Assisi. Clare, having once used the phrase "a little plant" to describe her rapport with Francis, unwittingly contributed to maintaining the image of a passive woman totally dependent on the male leader and teacher for her identity. (The "little plant" description actually indicated that the monastery of San Damiano was a small foundation created by the larger enterprise of Francis when his order was still young, and its forms were fluid and open to innovation. The phrase was commonly used to describe Benedictine "daughter" monasteries founded by a larger abbey.)

Years of study influenced by feminist scholarship and diligent work on sources from that period have allowed Clare's person to emerge with clearer lines, with far more depth than previously imagined. Still, the desire to find the precise category for the friendship of these two saints continues to haunt us. Father-daughter, brother-sister, master-disciple, soul friend, spiritual lover, actual lover—these descriptions have currency in many narratives and dramatic portraits. What they shared was the mysterious and generous outpouring of God's Holy Spirit granting each a profound desire to live the teachings of Jesus without compromise. It is not easy to grasp this inner core of invisible grace. Yet, we keep trying to do just that.

Perhaps words are the wrong way to describe their relationship. Perhaps another medium can reveal the wonder of how they lived into their shared identity.

Johann Sebastian Bach composed fifteen Two-Part Inventions. They involve what is known as "imitative counterpoint" in which themes are traded back and forth between left and right hand imitating one another. Listening to these works we hear an implied harmony that is clear, sophisticated, and has a quality of being inevitable without, however, being predictable. More than any other composer, Bach gives us perfect balance. We hear in linear fashion (independent melodies played at the same time) and vertical fashion (harmony created or implied by these lines of melody) all at once. The perfection that Bach achieved in these contrapuntal Inventions is said by scholars and artists to form a perfect balance or "cross" between the vertical and horizontal.

Listening to any one of these Inventions we experience this profound fusion of light and dark, horizontal and vertical, major and minor keys. The melodies flow together and by turns they move towards each other and then turn away, moving to different registers and tonalities. At times they fuse in a heart-stopping moment of beauty. At other moments they fly to different heights or depths, but they never clash in discordant conflict. Francis and Clare lived that twinned melodic mystery to be mirrored centuries later by the music of Bach.

Perhaps, then, in the end we realize that these saints, in all of their mysterious humanity, gift us with the Spirit's own music.

Thomas Merton captured this "inscape" of spiritual reality in this passage from *Conjectures of a Guilty Bystander:*

> There are people one meets in books or in life whom one does not merely observe, meet or know. A deep resonance of one's entire being is immediately set up with the entire being of the other. (*Cor ad cor loquitor*—heart speaks to

heart in the wholesomeness of the language of music; true friendship is a kind of singing).

It is my hope that this book has allowed each reader to hear this music, this enchanting legacy of Assisi's sainted woman of light and song.

Acknowledgments

*I*thank John E. Isom, geographer and cartographer, who collaborated with Keith Warner, O.F.M. in the production of *Journey and Place: An Atlas of St. Francis* published by the Franciscan Press in 2003. I am grateful for the permission to add his map of the Assisi region and for the work he did to customize it to this book. Murray Bodo gifted me with the poem "St. Clare Writes a Rule of Life" many years ago. Jean-François Godet-Calogeras played a crucial role in the production of my first thesis. His superb chronologies were a mainstay in this work. I am indebted to Richard Danielpour for masterful guidance regarding the Bach Inventions described in the Afterword.

The foundations for this biography have been strengthened by the work of many modern Franciscan scholars. Regis Armstrong took the torch of Clare studies from the great Ignatius Brady, OFM, and has spent a lifetime insuring our access to the primary Clarian sources in his volumes by Paulist Press, the Franciscan Institute, and New City Press. My teacher at the Institute and the Antonianum in Rome, he deserves my abundant thanks for insisting that I do this work when my own designs would have sent me in other directions. Andre Cirino, OFM, author teacher *par excellence,* shared that Roman sojourn with a friendship that continues to this day. The theology faculty of Duquesne University was a lifeline for my extended graduate studies on "the Bluff."

Once opened, the doors of Franciscan research never close. One finds companions along the way who offer extraordinary guidance and sharpen one's ability to avoid dangerous detours. My privileged friendships with Maria Pia Alberzoni, Jacques Dalarun, Marco Bartoli, + Raphael Pazzelli, Mike Higgins, Joseph Chinnici and the editors of the *Early Documents* volumes, Bill Short and Wayne Hellmann, have made the journey rich beyond all telling.

And the women......

The late Ingrid Peterson's biography and leadership of Clarefest '93; Joanne Schatzlein with Bill Hugo, OFM Cap, authored a new workbook, *Studying the Life of St. Clare of Assisi;* Frances Teresa Downing, OSC created four volumes of essays published by TAU Press. These added so much. Lezlie Knox, Darlene Pryds, and Catherine Mooney offer new analytic frameworks within the academy. My thanks for their continuing work.

+Ed Coughlin, OFM, as Director of the Franciscan Institute created the first Poor Clare Study sessions and produced a series of publications in honor of the 1993 anniversary. He modeled the "care and solicitude" that Francis enjoined on his brothers. He also modeled the manner in which academic administrators can foster scholarship and its applications.

Finally, I invoke the memory of +Don Aldo Brunacci, Canon of the Cathedral of San Rufino in Assisi and *Padrone* of Casa Papa Giovanni XXIII. His erudition was matched by his enthusiastic mentoring. This meant correcting my faulty Italian and then promoting the translation of my work into that gorgeous language. Translating his memories of the rescue of Jewish refugees during World War II was a privileged bond of friendship with ever widening circles in Assisi and here at home. May his memory be blessed by future generations.

Franciscan Media is a nonprofit ministry of the Franciscan Friars of St. John the Baptist Province. Through the publication of spiritual books, *St. Anthony Messenger* magazine, and online media properties such as *Saint of the Day, Minute Meditations,* and *Faith & Family,* Franciscan Media seeks to share God's love in the spirit of St. Francis of Assisi. For more information, to support us, and to purchase our products, visit franciscanmedia.org.

Margaret Carney is a member of the Sisters of St. Francis of the Neumann Communities. Her education in theology and Franciscan studies took place at Duquesne University, the Franciscan Institute of St. Bonaventure University and the Pontifical University Antonianum in Rome. She served on the commission responsible for the revisions of the Rule of the Third Order Regular in 1982 and completed her research on the Rule of St. Clare in 1988. From 1999-2004 she was the Director of the Franciscan Institute and served as a founding member of the Commission on the Franciscan Intellectual Tradition. Her presidency of St. Bonaventure University began in 2004 and she retired from that post in 2016. She continues to serve as a lecturer and leader for Catholic higher education and Franciscan organizations of the United States.